LOST AND FOUND

A Daughter's Tale of Violence and Redemption

Babette Hughes

THE PERMANENT PRESS
SAG HARBOR, NY 11963

Library of Congress Cataloging-in-Publication Data

Hughes, Babette
    Lost & Found: A Daughter's Tale of Violence and Redemption
      p. cm.
    ISBN 1-57962-072-8
    1. Hughes, Babette, 1922-. 2. Parent and adult child--United
    States--Case studies. 3. Family--United States--Case studies.
    4. Violence--United States--Case studies. 5. Murder--United
    States--Case studies. I. Title: Lost and Found. II. Title

    HQ755.86.H84 2000
    306.85'0973--dc21   99-057097
                                         CIP

September, 2000 - first printing

THE PERMANENT PRESS
4170 Noyac Road
Sag Harbor, NY 11963

For J. D

ACKNOWLEDGEMENTS

I'm grateful to my brother, Kenneth Rawson, who shared some of the years I have written about on these pages, and who read and confirmed the truth of them. And to Gary Polster, author of *Inside Looking Out: The Cleveland Jewish Orphan Asylum, 1868-1924*, who also read the manuscript for veracity,

Thanks, also, to my children, Eric, Steve, and Lisa for their support, and to Rosa and Debra for their caring.

Dennis Jarrett has my appreciation for his editing and friendship, as well as Richard Derus, who pointed the way.

My thanks to Betsy Friedlander, Toby Rawson, Ellen Aiello, Dorothy Braude, Doris Goldheimer, and Irene Sammet for their belief.

And finally, firstly and forever, I thank my husband, J. D. Hughes. Without his generous and loving encouragement, this book surely would never have been written. Not in a million years.

Why is it so new, why is this worn-out thing, death,
someone dying, so new so new?

Jamaica Kincaid

Here's how it's arranged
The heart can be repossessed
the liver, too,
and each single finger and toe.

Wistawa Szymborska

PREFACE

WHEN I WAS IN first grade Miss Charlton (whom we called Charlie because of her mustache) marched us into the auditorium to learn "My Country 'Tis of Thee." She sat down at the piano and led us through the song word by word, playing the piano with one hand and directing us with the other. When we came to the phrase "Land where my father died," I couldn't figure out how they all *knew*. At home my father's death was this big secret. There wasn't even a photograph of him anywhere, as if a picture could suddenly whisper the truth. Since all the other kids had fathers I reasoned it must be *my* father who died on the land they were singing about.

He vanished without a trace of the ordinary clutter and details of a life, leaving not a shadow nor footprint. There were no letters or insurance papers or tax receipts to find. Not a watch or drivers' license or birth certificate or deed to a house. No marriage license or diploma. No fading photograph that he had carried, maybe of me. Not a wedding portrait or snapshot at the beach. It was as if during the 29 years of his life on earth he was already a ghost.

My mother was as adamantly tight-lipped about my father as she was about everything else in her life. A walking, seething repository of secrets, she was willfully mute about her childhood, her husband, her marriage, and the secrets of her long widowhood.

So I embarked on a search not only for a father I never knew, but for my mother, who turned out to be even more of a mystery.

Although she never spoke of her 12 years in an orphanage, I learned of its horrors from reading *Inside Looking Out: The Cleveland Jewish Orphan Asylum,*

1868 to 1924 by Gary Edward Polster. *The Rise and Fall of the Cleveland Mafia* by Rick Porrello gave me details of my father's bootlegging activities, including events, dates, places and names. I read the family history my brother, Kenny, wrote after interviewing our relatives, as well as the lengthy newspaper accounts of our father's murder.

Kenny, old enough to remember him first-hand, told me of his charm, violent temper, and generosity. My mother's sister talked to me about their marriage; a cousin remembered the night he and Uncle Addie were killed. Another aunt related details of the funeral; an uncle told me stories about his vitality and lust and ambition. And they all knew who his killer was.

I was given a few pictures. In one, my father is a dark-eyed child on a tricycle. Another shows a muscular youth standing with his brother, Marvin, in front of a horse and delivery wagon from the family bakery. The picture is slightly out of focus, his grin blurred, but you can see his physical strength and his readiness to use it. In another he stands serenely in a handsome tan suit looking for all the world like a gentleman of banking or the law. His lips are thick and sensual, his eyes deep set. He is a beautiful young man.

He wears this same tan suit on a date with my mother. It is probably 1915 or 1916. In my family it does not seem strange that I don't know when my parents met, or even the month and year of their marriage. I come to this estimate by counting backwards from my brother's birth. My father is 20 in 1915 (I know this from the date inscribed on his tombstone), my mother, 18. I do know—or think I know—that they met at the Elysium, an indoor ice skating rink located in Cleveland at the corner of Euclid Avenue and 107th St.

He dresses carefully for his date. The tan suit and vest, a high stiff collar, a hat. His tie is silk, his wingtips gleam. He looks in the mirror and tilts his skimmer to a jaunty angle, tucks his gold watch in his waistcoat pocket, arranges the chain, and after another look in the glass pounds down the stairs.

When he arrives at my mother's, the neighbors peek through their curtains at his Winton, and five or six children gather around and touch its gleaming black surface. He gets out of the car, reaches in his pocket and gives each of them a dime. He squeezes the horn, summoning my mother. He squeezes it again. He leans against the door, jiggling his leg. His energy crackles the air. It makes passersby look up and shopkeepers stare and whisper. He is a magnetic field. He paces up and down the sidewalk. He shoos the children away who are now climbing all over the automobile. Suddenly he starts pounding urgently on my mother's door as if his energy will implode if he doesn't expend it on something, somewhere. He burns. He makes you hot. In my dreams I see him emanating a glow, wired by his own power.

Finally my mother comes out. He takes her arm and almost runs with her to the car. She smells of soap and Coty's powder from its flowered box. She is wearing her sister Mabel's good blue dress and her mother's feathered hat. When Mabel and Anna find out, there will be hell to pay, but now my mother is smiling. Aware of the neighbors' stares, she proudly lets herself be handed into the splendid automobile by Mr. Lou Rosen.

Did this—and what follows—really happen the way I have written it? Did everyone do what I say they did— think these thoughts and speak these words? I believe so. But it doesn't really matter, not to me, because I have absorbed so many reports and whispers and been told so many confessions and recollections for so long that they have become part of me and are as fixed as the moon.

One

I HAVE A blurred mental image of my mother coming home from my daddy's funeral. She is wearing a veiled black hat that scares me. I am two years old and had been left at home, put to bed for my nap by a big colored lady. But I can't sleep. The house feels too quiet. Something big is wrong. I stand up in my crib and scream. No one comes.

Finally I am taken downstairs. Grown-ups in dark clothes are standing around whispering. There is the cloying smell of sweet pastries, the sound of china; ladies in aprons are busy in the kitchen. One of them gives me a cookie. She is crying. I have never seen a grown-up cry before and I start to wail. A man picks me up; his face feels scratchy. I scramble down and look for my mother.

I see her sitting in a big chair and run to her. She pulls me onto her lap. I tug at the black veil knocking off her hat but, still, I cannot stop crying. "Babette, honey, shh, don't cry, it's all right," she murmurs. I feel her heart pound through my dress and, weeping, hang onto her until someone wipes my runny nose and pulls me away.

My mother sits quietly in the big chair listening to the noises of the kitchen and the murmur of the mourners' voices. Hearing a piercing screech she thinks it came from her own mouth. But no one turns to her and she realizes it was a screaming tea kettle. She stares at the mourners in their dark clothes and sorrowful faces as they move about the dining room table laden with platters of herring, smoked whitefish, smoked salmon, cream cheese, hard-boiled eggs, bagels and Kaiser rolls. Home-made sponge cake, macaroons and fig newtons, baked by the ladies in the kitchen while her husband was being buried.

Upstairs, my daddy's suits hang limply with their empty sleeves, neatly arranged by color and season, the dark blues and grays giving way along the rack to the summer creams and whites. Shallow drawers hold rows of jeweled cuff links, a rainbow of ties stretches along a wall, and dozens of stiff-collared silk shirts hang neatly in whites and pastels.

Now the mourners are filling the large, proud living room after first washing their hands from the pitcher on the front stoop. (Someone had set up the ancient Jewish funeral ritual as if this were a benign death and you could wash off the wreckage.) My mother looks around for my brother, a tow-headed blue-eyed boy of six, but he has already escaped into the backyard our daddy had equipped with swings, jungle gyms, even a child-sized car. Peering through the window she sees him riding his car on the hard, gray snow, his correct little tie off and already a rip in the scratchy suit jacket bought especially for his father's funeral.

Earlier, at the burial, he had dutifully thrown a small handful of dirt into the freshly dug grave as the rabbi muttered the Kaddish. I see him there in the shimmer of a dream and imagine heat rays emanating from the open grave like the disturbed air of hell. Suddenly my mother's knees buckle under her. The funeral director with his neat, black suit and blank eyes reaches out and steadies her with the expressionless efficiency of his profession, corpses and collapsing widows as unremarkable to him as an accountant's pencil and adding machine. Her dizziness is actually due to the pill given her by a Dr. Magio who is said to be kept on a retainer for the time a bullet or two has to be discreetly removed, and who was called when my mother was unable to stop screaming. She feels shame in her near-collapse and extravagant sorrow—mixed as it is with a curious and confusing measure of relief that Lou Rosen's vitality and violence are now subdued six feet under. She is only 27 after all, her flesh still young, her thighs still slender and surely not meant never to open to a man again.

But if she imagines freedom and options with a pounding heart she learns soon enough that the dead do not leave. Even without the lingering scent of his after-shave, the damp towel across the bed, the diamond stick pin and gold cuff links on the bedside table, Lou is an ongoing gauzy presence, everywhere and nowhere, hovering over her, over all of us.

Now, sitting in the living room, my mother watches a group of three men as they enter her house and hang up their coats and fedoras on the racks provided by the Berkowitz Funeral Home. She knows that the big man, the one with the drooping eyelids and heavy glasses, ordered her husband's murder—she wonders if the two men with him were the actual killers. She also knows that the hundreds of white carnations and roses covering his casket were sent by their polite murdering hands. But she is not afraid; she has been a bootlegger's wife long enough to know that as long as they keep their silence widows and children are sacrosanct. She has been a bootlegger's wife long enough to understand the code; no one will harm her unless, of course, she breaks it and reveals his name, which she knows to be Joe Lonardo, the Cleveland Mafia boss who is now offering his clean hand to her in solemn-faced sympathy. She shakes his hand and feels her stomach rise to her throat. She is afraid she will vomit on his wingtips.

The rabbi in his black suit and beard and woeful expression is standing with Marvin, brother of the deceased. Marvin has thick black hair that looks wind-blown, or mussed from making love. Talking to the rabbi, gesturing with his hands, he is smiling as if he's at a wake with believers of an afterlife, even for Lou Rosen. The rabbi is eating a wedge of sponge cake. He wipes his mouth with a dinky embroidered napkin. There are crumbs in his beard. He puts his empty plate down on the grand piano, straightens his *yarmulke*, and crosses the room to my mother. He leans over and kisses her on the cheek; she feels his beard brush her face and has an impulse to grab hold of it. She feels like laughing and has to duck her head and hold her handkerchief to her mouth.

"Mrs. Rosen—are you all right?" the rabbi asks. His voice is deep, concerned.

She nods. She even smiles. She wonders if she is going crazy. Although the rabbi is older than she by at least a decade, she thinks he is too young to have anything to say to her. She wants him to go away, to leave her alone. But he sits down in a chair at her side, looks into her eyes and speaks. What? What did he say? She is too preoccupied to hear. She wants to ask him if her husband killed anyone before he was killed; if God had punished him, an eye for an eye. She wants to ask him if a bootlegger can get into heaven. Or a boot-legger's wife, for that matter. She wants to ask him if there is a heaven. She wants to ask him if there is a God. Foolish woman! Not a question for a rabbi. But the truth is she receives little comfort from his respectful atten-dance or his pieties or from the funeral service or the Kaddish her son, a child of six, had dutifully repeated in a clear child's voice at graveside, and has no hope of heavenly intervention into the life she has already found to be absurd. Sitting there, receiving condolences, she feels that God is unaware of her small mistaken exis-tence and that it would be dangerous to get the attention of such a capricious deity who maybe has it in for orphan girls who get mixed up with gangsters. So she says nothing as the rabbi rises to leave, lowering her eyes and retreating into the hushed respect reserved for the newly widowed.

She notices her mother sitting across the room. When did she come in? Anna Wolf (Wolf being her second husband, now dead, who was said to have given her the syphilis that eventually killed her) is sitting on the couch with her purse on her knees. She has good bones, the same good bones as my mother, her face is sculptured like an aristocrat's, and with her haughty bearing, could have been reincarnated from a former blue-blooded life. She is daintily eating a cookie with her pinky finger held aloft, sipping from her cup as if she were at a tea party. Now she puts the cup down on the coffee table, opens her purse, retrieves a mirror and tube of lipstick, and carefully applies it to her thin mouth with her reddened arthritic fingers. I do not like the feel of my grandmother's dry rough hands on my skin.

Anna's first husband was Jacob Smith, the name changed from Schmitko when he emigrated to Cleveland from Poland. But his new Americanized name and youth, his grand handlebar mustache and his young wife couldn't protect him from the tuberculosis epidemic—known in those days as consumption. He died at the age of thirty after a long illness leaving Anna with nothing but four children, a meager grocery store, and her own cold heart.

Tending to her few customers, she left her small daughters to the streets of the Scovil Avenue neighborhood. That is, until the day a neighbor paid a visit to the authorities and reported Anna Smith's appalling neglect of her three little girls, who, dirty and hungry, had been running wild in the neighborhood for weeks, months. My mother, Florence, was 3; her sisters, Lillian and Mabel, 5 and 7.

Soon after, a high-bosomed woman and a man with a walrus mustache and a watch chain showed up at

Anna's grocery store. She led them upstairs to her rooms, telling her daughters to wait outside. They sat down obediently on the stoop in their grimy, torn dresses. A peddler passed, rattling his cart filled with pots and pans. It was July, and the air smelled of garbage, urine and the cabbage from someone's kitchen. A baby was crying overhead and a woman leaned out of her window calling to her son, who was nowhere in sight. After awhile, the man emerged folding papers into his breast pocket. He nodded to the woman waiting on the stoop with the children and one at a time she lifted the three ragged girls into the wagon. (Della, too young at six months to be taken, was left upstairs with Anna.) Florence, my mother, started to scream as if she was the only one who understood what was happening, setting off her sisters. The woman reached in her bag and gave each weeping child a small lollipop. Even though their mother had a grocery store and a glass jar of penny candy stood on the dusty shelf, they were never given any, and they stopped crying, tore off the wrapper and began sucking greedily. The man and woman climbed into the wagon as the neighbors stared through their windows; the man jiggled the horse's reins, and it disappeared, rattling down the cobblestone street.

In my sentimental imagination I picture Anna running after the horse and wagon, arms outstretched, tears streaming down her face, crying, My babies! My babies! Like in a silent movie. Like Charlie Chaplin and Jackie Coogan in *The Kid*. But I know better. What I know of Anna is that she turned away to wait on a customer. Or simply stood watching them leave from her window.

When they arrived at the Jewish Orphan Asylum on Woodland Avenue and 55th street, a smell of rot rose from the earth. The sisters stared at the high iron-spiked fence that surrounded the large buildings, the barred windows and the ragged children watching them from the playground. Sobbing in fear, they eyed still another frightening stranger come toward them on this bewildering morning. Later they would learn that he was Dr. Sam Wolfenstein, the director, whom they would come to regard with fear and awe as a surrogate for God himself, with his heavy beard and bushy eyebrows, weekly sermons, strict discipline and constant admonitions about the moral life.

"Now, now," he said, lifting my mother, the smallest, out of the wagon. "You'll have to stop that crying."

But she didn't. She was three years old but she knew that something very bad was happening; the disappearance of her mother, her lollipop and her freedom all tangled together into a confusing sense of terrifying loss. She couldn't stop crying. She could not.

"Hush!" he said, louder.

But his shouts only brought forth a fresh cascade of screams.

"Stop it! This minute!" he shouted, unused to being disobeyed by his orphans. He held her small, dirty, screaming self at arms-length like a bad-smelling, noisy, squirming chicken and handed her to the woman from the wagon. As she took their screaming baby sister away, Mabel and Lill watched wide-eyed, their terror and confusion striking them mute.

The sisters were then separated into their respective age groups among the other 500 "inmates" (as they were called in their lives behind bars) enduring yet another loss—this time of each other.

My mother was taken to a large damp room in the basement (infested, like the orphanage's other nineteenth-century buildings, with huge rats, lice and bedbugs). Staring with alarm at the large pool of green water with two ladders leading down into it, she was stripped and examined for lice. The probing of her head and body by yet another stranger set her off again into a rejuvenated fit of wailing until she was dragged into the tub and shocked into silence by the scalding water. After being scrubbed by one of the older girls, her hair was cut off—setting off a lifelong preoccupation with her hair. (Over the years, following the fashion of the day, she had it bobbed, upswept, permed, straightened, marcelled, streaked, layered.)

Scrubbed, de-loused, and shorn, exhausted and subdued, she was now put into thick, gray undergarments with long legs that itched winter and summer. Black stockings went on next, then a red flannel underskirt and finally a dress of wool that reached the ankles. Over that went a blue striped apron. Shoes were made of thick leather that laced up over the ankles. After being dressed she was assigned a number that was sewn on her uniform and by which she was henceforth known.

She was always hungry. While doing her dawn-to-dusk chores, during her hours of Hebrew and Bible study, she was hungry. Attending classes in German, English and mathematics, history, social studies and geography, penmanship and spelling, she was hungry. Sitting among the five hundred other orphans at long wooden tables of ten in enforced silence, there was never enough to eat, and for every hour of each and every day, for the next twelve years, she was hungry.

But she was also smart, every year performing academically at the top of her class. And at the age of fifteen, on a lovely June afternoon in 1912, my mother graduated valedictorian from the Jewish Orphan Home.

After the ceremonies, her Hebrew teacher, Mrs. Adler, climbed the stairs to her dorm where my mother was packing her few belongings. "You're to go to the office," she told her.

Clutching her valedictorian medal, she ran downstairs. Mrs. Goldstein, the secretary, was standing in the administration office with a woman Florence had never seen before.

"This is Anna Smith," Mrs. Goldstein said. "She is your mother." Florence stared at the stranger standing there in a brown coat and feather-trimmed hat. Anna Smith had never visited her daughters. Not once. Not once in 12 years.

But my mother went home with Anna—where else could she go? Her older sisters, Mabel and Lill, had preceded her, and their small apartment was so crowded the last one home had to sleep on the floor and the second one up in the morning got the last of the two pairs of silk stockings they owned among them.

Although Anna hadn't showed up at the Home, she came to the house after the funeral that day, sitting silently and drinking her tea and applying lipstick with the monumental indifference her daughter envied but could not, for the life of her, emulate. Her own passions had led her from the orphan's cloistered world to the bootlegger's life, and she might have looked at her strange mother receiving polite condolences with wonder and rage. Growing up, I heard her cheerfully, guiltlessly and frequently announce that she hated her mother. Which embarrassed me. It made me nervous. You just weren't supposed to say you hated your own mother. And yet she was a dutiful daughter, taking her in to live with us during the Depression, giving her money at no small sacrifice, going on streetcars to visit her in bitter cold weather after she moved out. I guess she was still trying to have a mother. Even Anna.

Two

I AM THIRTY-THREE years old and I am sitting in a psychiatrist's waiting room, wondering what I'm doing here. I am a good suburban wife. I have three children, a beautiful home, a rich husband. I am fortunate. So why am I waiting for a psychiatrist with a *Time* magazine in my wet palms that I'm too nervous to read? I do not know. Or I do know. It is my baffling misery. It is my confusion. It is because my husband tells me frequently that I'm stupid. Also crazy. It is because I believe him.

I open the magazine on my lap. There is a full-page ad for a Chrysler, the same color and model as ours. It reminds me of the night Nate pushed me out of it on our way home from a party.

As soon as we got in the car that night I saw he was furious about something. "What's wrong?" I asked.

"What's wrong?" he imitated in a singsong.

"What did I do?"

"You're so stupid I have to tell you what you did? I told you not to wear that dress!"

"But . . ."

"I told you not to wear it and you snuck out with it under your coat. Then you act like a dumb jackass, talking to Chuck Stern who you know I can't stand. Don't think I didn't see you flirting with him. And with Al Whatshisname, hanging on his every word like he's the Messiah or something." He turned to me with the same self-righteous look on his face as the night we first met at Lenny Adelson's party, when he slipped my date a Mickey and made Bob so dizzy and sick he had to pull over to the side of the road on the way home and throw up out the window. "Then you go and let that idiot Arnie put on your boots!" he went on. "I saw him looking down your dress. I saw him. I told you not to wear that goddamn thing."

I was beginning to understand. I hadn't spent enough time at his side. Or worn that damn tweed suit. Unable somehow to defend myself, choking with unexpressed protest, sick of his accusations, sick of his rage, sick of him, all I wanted was to get away. "Let me out of here!" I yelled.

He reached across, opened the door and pushed me out of the moving car. I landed in a snow bank. The car hadn't been going very fast and I got up, brushed off the snow and looked around. We were on our street. I could see him pulling into our driveway.

I walked home. Inside, Nate was sitting in the family room. "I want a divorce," I said.

"What is it with you? Every time we have a fight you want a divorce."

I went to a lawyer the next day, a different one this time. He successfully discouraged me the way the last one had, which, thinking of my children, was easy to do. So once again, I knuckled under. Besides, Nate usually behaved better for awhile after I threatened divorce, and I always made myself believe the change would last.

But just this morning he stormed into the kitchen and shook the Halle bill in my face. "I make the money and you spend it? Is that how it works?"

I took the bill from his fist and looked at it. "Nate, a pair of shoes."

"Yeah, shoes. Last month, a dress. What the hell do you do with the money I give you?"

"Groceries and—" I stopped. I was guilty. I slipped my mother money from my household allowance.

"Take the shoes back," he ordered.

It was my fault. I forgot to ask his permission before I bought them. He was actually generous. Very generous. He bought me jewels—diamonds, emeralds, real pearls. He liked to go shopping with me, he liked to pick out my clothes. But he didn't like my buying anything without his okay.

I didn't protest. How could I? He was generous, I was guilty; I even felt guilty for my misery, as if I was being punished for committing some unknown crime in a dream. I observed myself with curiosity, perfectly aware that this wasn't normal. I should fight back, defend myself, point out that he didn't need *my* permission for his cashmere jackets and custom made suits; his expensive cameras and golf clubs and tennis rackets. Antiques and paintings. (Our art collection was written up in the *Cleveland Plain Dealer*.) The 55-foot yacht and the captain he kept year round on full salary in Ft. Lauderdale, the first class travel to four star hotels and world class restaurants. I should scream, throw things, weep. I wondered, is this how people go crazy? Calmly, quietly, going numb?

The next time I went to the supermarket I wrote down the cost of everything I bought; milk, eggs, coffee, bread, pot roast, bananas, apples, lettuce, cereal, tea, ham, bacon, peanut butter, canned soup, hamburger, carrots, potatoes. But that night when I showed it to him with each price neatly itemized, he waved it away without looking, like a king irritated with his subject's pathetic efforts to please.

So I figured if I were only smarter or nicer or more careful; if I could somehow become a better wife, mother, person; if I could figure out what I was doing wrong instead of always being blind-sided, Nate wouldn't have such shouting scorn for me. Clearly, I had to change. So when I asked my doctor to recommend a psychiatrist, all I wanted was to become a woman who didn't fill her husband with contempt.

"Good afternoon," Dr. Herman says, startling me. He holds the door open. "Please come in."

I get up and enter his office. Following me, he shuts

the door and walks around to his chair behind the desk. I stand in the middle of the room. I hear the radiator hiss. I eye the couch. Am I supposed to lie down? I want to run out of there.

"Please," he says, indicating the chair facing his desk. He has dark hair, eyeglasses, and looks to be in his mid-fifties. I think I had been expecting someone more exotic, maybe with a beard, maybe a Viennese accent, because I am faintly surprised to be looking at the mild even-featured face of a man you'd see on the bus or working in a bank. Even the room has an anonymous look with its leather couch, ordinary desk and chair. The light is muted, the pictures on the wall unobtrusive, dull even (a pastoral scene of sky and barn, a seascape, a still life of fruit and flowers) as if nothing is permitted to distract from whatever it is that goes on in here.

He looks at me, waiting.

I sit down. But I don't know what to say. How can this stranger help me when I don't even know what's wrong? I decide to escape this shadowy, barren room. I'll tell him I've made a mistake coming here and leave so he can treat someone who needs him.

"What can I do for you?" he asks.

Uttered by a psychoanalyst the cliche suddenly takes on weight. What can he do for me? What can he do for *me*? Was someone actually offering help who maybe even knows how? And to my astonishment and chagrin I start to cry, the tears beginning somewhere way behind my eyes, my soul, stored up like heat in some deep unknown region of my being, mysteriously released by this quiet, calm stranger in this unknown room. Tears fall down my face in a torrent. I weep in embarrassment and relief. He hands me the box of Kleenex from his desk and sits silently while I blow my nose and mop up my face.

"What made you sad?" he asks.

I shrug. I am afraid I'll start crying again.

He asks a few questions—ordinary questions that anyone might ask, except his are quieter, almost gentle, like a doctor probing a sore abdomen: Does this hurt? Does this? This? Answering, I find myself talking about my misery and confusion.

"Our time's almost up," he says, "and we need to discuss your treatment—what kind, when, the fees, and so forth."

"What kind?"

"I think you would profit more from analysis than therapy."

"What's the difference?"

"Well, therapy is a narrower approach, sessions are once or twice a week usually for a limited period. Analysis goes far deeper, with sessions every day. It takes much longer, too—usually no less than three years and often more. Also, analysts are medical doctors who have had to be analyzed themselves. They then go through two additional years of training and another period of supervised work with patients."

"What do you do?" I am beginning to like this guy.

"I do both."

"Okay, analysis then."

He leans back in his chair. "How do you feel about a daily commitment?"

I don't know how I feel about anything. "Okay."

"My fee is $25 a session. How do you feel about that?"

$125 a week was a lot of money back then. But I know how I feel about that. "It's only money," I say.

He opens his appointment book. "Can you come from 5 to 5:50?"

I nod. My housekeeper always cooked dinner anyway. Still, I didn't like the idea of being away from the children after school. "Is there any other time?"

He shakes his head. "As it is I'm lengthening my day. I usually quit at five."

"Will you move me if another time opens up?"

"Certainly," he says, getting up. "See you tomorrow." We shake hands and I leave.

Driving home I feel a wave of something like release. Dr. Herman is an utter stranger; I have no idea how this analysis works or even *if* it works; but for the first time in my life I don't feel all alone.

When I told Nate I had decided to go into analysis I expected a fight, but he surprised me. "Go ahead and waste your time if you want." He narrowed his eyes; "Just get this straight. I'm not paying for it."

"Okay," I said. I'd manage from my household allowance.

No one I knew or heard of back then was seeing a psychiatrist, or if they were—as I discovered years later—like me, they didn't confess. Besides, seeing a psychiatrist was another sign of my failure to be like other people, a secret mysteriously connected to the murders, and it made me ashamed. So I didn't tell anyone else except my mother. She answered with a comment I've remembered all of my life. "Let me know when you find out what a son of a bitch I was."

The next day I find myself standing uncertainly in the middle of Dr. Herman's office. The room with its couch along the wall now seems as familiar and strange as a place you see in a dream. I watch him settle himself in a chair behind the couch. (Why hadn't I noticed the chair there before?) He sits, waiting. I get the idea and gingerly lie down on the couch, carefully tucking my skirt under my knees.

He is behind me now, out of my vision. The room fills with silence. It is in an old building with high ceilings, wood floors, radiators. I can hear the creaky elevator. I smell his piney aftershave. Overhead, someone in high heels walks briskly across a bare floor. I stare at the ceiling. I don't know what to say. I lie there feeling ridiculous.

"Just relax and say whatever comes to mind," Dr. Herman prompts.

But I lie there, mute. He sits behind me, making me nervous. I want to escape this room, this silent, waiting stranger.

"I don't think I know how to do this," I finally say, thinking Nate's right, this is a waste of time. I have nothing to say to this person I hear breathing behind me.

"What are you thinking?" he asks.

"Nothing," I lie.

Silence.

I need him to say something. Anything. "Am I supposed to tell you my dreams?"

"Dreams are helpful," he says.

"I don't remember my dreams," I say. Another lie. I've got to get out of here.

"Well then, tell me about your family."

"My mother's a secretary, my brother's vice president of sales for a paper company in New York. I have three children, two boys, Lewis and Andrew, and a baby girl."

"What about your father?"

"I told you about him yesterday."

He sits in his chair diabolically waiting for me to stir up buried skeletons and banished ghosts. But I joined my mother in silence about my father years ago.

"I don't want to talk about him," I finally say.

"Okay, what about your husband?"

"What?"

"Well, you mentioned your mother, father, brother and children, but not your husband."

"His name's Nate."

"What's he like?"

"Nate? Oh, Nate's very talented—he's won prizes for his photography, you know. He's a city councilman and he runs one of the biggest auto agencies in Ohio and he's an expert gardener—all our friends come to him for advice—oh, and he's a gourmet cook. He has a great sense of humor, too—he likes to play practical jokes on people." (I don't tell him how mean the jokes can be.)

"How do you you feel about him?"

"I just told you."

"That's not what I asked."

"How do I feel about him? Fine. I feel fine."

I hear him stir in his seat. "Babette, why did you come here?"

"I came because—" I stop. "See, there's nothing wrong with Nate. I just told you. It's me who's a mess. He's always criticizing me. That's why I'm here. To find out how to change. Isn't that what psychiatrists do?"

"And what do you do?"

"What do I do?"

"When he criticizes you. What do you do?"

"Nothing."

"Nothing? You don't defend yourself?"

"No, we never fight."

"Why not?"

"I told you! Because it's always my fault!"

"What's your fault?"

I am crying. "I don't know."

"We need to work on that," he says, handing me the box of Kleenex.

"Work on what?"

"On why you feel so guilty."

I breathe. "See, Nate's a good provider."

"A good provider?"

"Well, yeah. I have, you know, a house, food, clothes." My words vibrate in my ears. I feel my face heat up. "Listen," I say, "it's not how that sounds."

"How does it sound?"

"Oh, as if I'm like begging for my room and board like a waif or something."

Silence.

"Is that what you think?" I demand.

"You're the one who said it, not me."

"Well, it's absurd."

"You sound angry."

Cowering for my keep? Subservience for room and board? No way. I made no such bargain.

"Our time's up," he says.

I rise to my feet and slam out of there.

Three

AFTER MY DADDY'S funeral; after my mother sat *shiva* for the ritual week with the mirrors covered and the radio turned off; after receiving streams of visitors with their murmured condolences and suffering the presence of the rabbi at her side who smelled of something sour, like pickles, she closed and locked the door to the last visitor. Then she threw out the vases of dying flowers and baskets of uneaten, decaying fruit that had begun to smell of rot. Shedding her black dress, she gave her veiled hat to the maid, bobbed her hair and started running so fast and far it was as if she didn't want to know what had already happened. She never returned to her husband's sad, fresh grave, letting it get sunken and untended over the years, unvisited, shaggy with weeds.

My mother went downtown and came home with a red dress, high-heeled rhinestone and satin shoes, a flirtatious red hat, and two evening gowns in clinging fabrics. Opening the boxes on the couch, she shook out the tissue paper, lifted the fringed red dress to her chin and twirled around the living room. She was so abruptly transformed from the grieving widow of only hours ago it was as if she had sipped some kind of magic potion that buried Lou Rosen's mourning wife along with him. Her soft mouth hardened, her brows lifted as if in surprise, her face slipped from mournful to provocative, her body from its defeated slump to defiant flesh. She even smelled different; like musk, like sex. People—the maid, my aunts—whispered.

Disappearing in unpredictable spurts, she sent Kenny and me separately to a series of aunts and uncles: Aunt Mabel and Uncle Red (for his red hair), Aunt Lill and Uncle Sanford, Aunt Sally and Uncle Sid, Aunt

30

Linda and Uncle Marvin, Aunt Milly and Uncle Doc (a veterinarian), Aunt Goldie and Uncle Myron.

Aunt Goldie was always cleaning her house. People, even grown-ups, had to take off their shoes to come in. Her preoccupation with dirt added to my humiliation the mornings I woke up in a wet bed and had to watch her wrinkle her nose as she whipped off the sheets. I wanted to help in my shame, but she waved me away and dashed from the room holding the sheets at arms length as if they were on fire. It was an exercise poor Aunt Goldie had to endure often; away from my mother I was a bed wetter. I sat on the floor at the foot of my stripped-down bed in my wet pajamas and embarrassment, shut my eyes, and pretended that my mother was downstairs waiting to take me home.

I remember wonderful food at Aunt Milly's, who, demonstrating that my memory of her table is no mere fantasy, later actually opened a restaurant. But I loved the food at my other aunts' too, even when I didn't, even when it wasn't good. I accepted seconds and asked politely for thirds. Then I finished the meal with three slices of bread swathed with butter, while my cousins stared at me and squirmed in their chairs, their carrots and hamburgers and mashed potatoes scarcely touched. (I had all I could do not to clean up their plates, too.) Watching me approvingly, my aunts thought they were great cooks. They didn't know that every time my mother left me, I felt hollowed out with a huge cavity I couldn't fill.

Uncle Red built a thrilling puppet stage for my cousin Judy and me that had real curtains you could close with a string. But Aunt Mabel, who was excitable and angry, often flew into terrifying rages. Once when she screamed at Kenny for something or other, he ran away. He took me with him. I was four years old and he was nine. We hid in the woods. All I remember is my feeling of pride being pulled along by my big brother.

31

And my fear. I have no idea how long we were in the woods, it could have been an hour or a day, but I seem to see a chalk-white sky slowly turning darker and thick trees casting ominous shadows, scaring me. Kenny was holding my hand but I began to cry anyway, which may be how we were finally found.

My aunts were friendly enough, although somewhat falsely friendly, I thought, with a child's canny perception. Still, they were friendlier than their children, my cousins, who were expected to play with the well-behaved interloper that I was. Look at Babbie's clean plate, my aunts said to their children. See her nice manners; look how quietly she plays, how she minds without back-talk and sass; see how she eats her vegetables and notice that she doesn't leave a mess. Why can't you be like that? No wonder my cousins didn't like me. But it was better than getting on a grown-up's nerves and thrown out. My mother seemed as remote and sparkling and mysterious as the night sky and I didn't know if she would come back for me. Waiting, I felt disconnected, in space, somewhere outside the world; in my mother's sweet-smelling fleshy presence I was grounded again, saved. Nights in my aunts' houses, in their beds, I still smelled her, felt her breath. She seemed to reside in my brain and lurk in the air. I wanted to disappear into her rustling clothes, I wanted to vanish into her body, into her womb again; I wanted to become her.

Summers she took me to Aunt Mabel's in Rye, New York, or Aunt Lill's in Boston, driving the five hundred miles over unpaved roads, gunning the accelerator with her high heeled sandal as if the future stretched ahead as free and open-ended as the road, and the past, receding in our rear view mirror, gone forever.

I caught the way the highway whispered to her of promise, and feeling blissful, feeling the warmth of her body, the vibration of the motor and my own utter contentment, I was saved. My mother was mine now, not mysteriously away somewhere, the two of us comrades of the road. Wrapped together in our little car, we were insulated and safe because my mother was brave and strong and my father was watching out for us from the black sky overhead.

She would stop for coffee at some all night diner or truck stop, a bright oasis of light in the dark, and I'd wake and stumble in with her, proud to be up so late with my mom in this grown-up night. There would be a few men scattered on the counter stools and she'd gulp the coffee from a thick white cup and hug her purse as if someone was about to snatch it away. Back in the car, riding with my head in her lap, she stroked my hair and sang to me in a thin soprano. "Mighty like a Rose," "Sleep Kentucky Babe," "Sweet and Low." Later, I wondered how she had learned lullabies in an orphanage.

As she sings to me, the car floats along the road and then it goes up up up into the sky. We are going to my daddy. It isn't night any more up there, the air is all pink, and I see a huge pointy castle drifting in the wind. I order my mom to take me to the castle because my daddy is in there and he's a king. She does what I say because I'm the boss and because she's my twin and we're holding hands. We leave our car with a clown and she carries me over a bridge into the castle. I see a king with a diamond crown on his head and gold robes. That's not your daddy, she says. I order her to put me down and I run to him. He has a bushy beard and mean eyes and he scares me. My mother hits him with a stick. I cry because he isn't my daddy. We look in all the rooms of the castle and then we see him. My daddy is in bed. He is very sick. My mother and I stay with him a long time until it gets dark and he falls asleep and the mean king comes into the room. When my mother sees him she grabs me and we run to the car. We leave the sky and go back to the ground. We're still holding hands. It's us against the mean king, us against the world.

As we drove, beams of light headed toward us and then vanished like the strange prehistoric creatures in my picture book. We slept in tourist homes, an adventure with the smiling host and strange bedroom, and arrived at my aunt's the next evening, stiff and happy. My mother and her sister drank coffee at the kitchen table and talked; I'd hear their voices while my cousin Judy and I played. But she always left two or three days later without me, and it always broke my heart. I would grow distracted, half there in my play, as if she had taken part of me away with her.

Still, she could turn up as suddenly as she had disappeared, and she came back, swooping me up in her arms, returning me to life with her smell, her musical voice, the feel of her body. She had rented another apartment, one of the fourteen we were to occupy during my childhood. I attended six different schools; three elementary: Fairfax, Prospect and Roxboro; two junior high: Roxboro and Roosevelt; and Heights High. Kenny, four-and-a-half-years older and starting earlier, attended ten.

This apartment was half way up a hill nestled in a row of other brick buildings just like it, with a string of garages along the back and a gas station on the corner. The rooms were on the third floor and sort of shadowy.

When my mother and I arrived home after our two-day trip, Kenny was just back from somewhere, too, playing outside. I dashed downstairs to see him. He grinned and waved as if he was glad to see me and I sat down on the stoop feeling content; my mother was upstairs in our apartment unpacking suitcases, Kenny was right here in front of me, our family was together again. It must have been summer because I was wearing shorts; I remember feeling the stoop's cold concrete on the back of my legs, and the thick smell of the honeysuckle vine that grew along the garage wall. I sat there watching Kenny play with Tommy Aspin.

I thought it was a game of cowboys and Indians, or cops and robbers, until I saw Kenny point his squirt gun at Tommy, yelling, "I'm my daddy and I'm gonna get you!"

He lowered his gun. "Tommy," he said with great disgust, "just shoot me. I told you, I'm my daddy. I get murdered. You have to shoot me."

Tommy squirted Kenny with his gun, shouting, "Bang bang!"

"They got me!" Kenny hollered, staggering around clutching his chest. He threw himself on the ground. "I'm dead!" he yelled.

"You boys stop that!" I yelled in my mother's voice from my perch on the stoop. "My daddy was not murdered!" Tommy looked at me, his face getting red. But my brother lay motionless on the ground with his eyes squeezed shut and his arms across his chest. I stared down at him. My daddy dead of murder? Not just plain dead like my friend Beverly's grandmother? Our kindergarten class had written a letter to Beverly's family and when she came back to school after the funeral she drew a picture of her mother with fat tears on her face and a turned-down mouth. Then her own eyes got all teary and she started to cry. Miss Bailey pulled Beverly on her lap and said it was okay to feel sad and cry when someone died. But I never saw my mother cry about my daddy. I never saw anyone even feel sad. Beverly said her grandmother was up in heaven, so I guessed my daddy was up there, too, with all the other dead people.

But maybe Kenny knew more than I did—he was, after all, almost 10. Suddenly I felt the same way I did the night I saw a bad man in my closet and woke screaming. My mother had come running. She said it was just a nightmare. But I couldn't fall back asleep until she stayed with me and kept a light on in my room.

I raced up the stairs. "Mommy! Kenny said Daddy was murdered!" I think I was crying.

She was unpacking a large suitcase. Putting an armload of clothes on the bed she sat down and pulled me onto her lap. "No no, Babbie. Kenny was just playing. Your father died of pneumonia."

I think I knew even then that Kenny was acting out the truth with a child's unblinking accuracy. But I swallowed my mother's story whole, and with relief.

I imagined her at my daddy's bedside, sponging his young, hot face, a good and devoted wife, taking his temperature, giving him pink baby aspirins and orange juice with one of those crooked straws I sucked on when I had the measles. He asked if he could see me—he wanted me to come and make him better because he loved me the best. But they wouldn't let me. I had my magic medicine all ready but they wouldn't let me give it to him. So he died while I was taking a special bath that he had gotten out of bed to make for me; it had big puffy bubbles like white balloons. Before, I was playing bridge with the colored lady because I was a very smart baby. My daddy knew I was. He didn't want to die and leave us but he had to. He had to go be the king.

My mother cried because she loved him and couldn't save him. Murder is just in storybooks. My father died of pneumonia. My mother said so.

And soon she was disappearing to mysterious places again, running again, as if she felt her husband's public shame stick to her like flypaper. Or maybe now that Lou was gone, now that the worst had happened, she felt an odd letdown. Wasn't it anticlimactic to dwell in ordi-

nary life without the old heart-stopping fear and excitement? Wasn't it more interesting to live on the edge or
in flight? Her newly bobbed hair cupped her head like a
helmet, she was as slender as a boy and as glamorous as
a movie star. All she had to do now was dress up in
beaded chiffon and swinging ropes of pearls and keep
moving. All she had to remember now was how to do
the Charleston and the Black Bottom and flirt and hold
her scotch.

If I squint my eyes I can see her in her bedroom of
pale satins and shimmering silks. After growing up in a
dormitory that slept 100 orphans, she is Cinderella;
bewitched, I watch her slip into a glittering dress, step
into her satin slippers, spray her slender neck with
perfume, drape her shoulders in mink. She kisses me
goodbye, scratching my cheek with her earring, and is
gone. Proud and sad, I stare at the closed door feeling a
sudden emptiness where she had stood, sparkling, only
moments before.

She was in such a good mood every time she left and
so quiet and sad at home, I started to worry. So the next
time I saw her with her hat and suitcase, I grabbed her
sleeve. I was crying. She told me to let go; she said
she'd be home soon. But I knew I'd never see her again
and I hung on. She pulled my hands off, hurting my
fingers. A quick hug and she was gone.

The next time I saw her getting ready to leave I
slipped outside, opened the back door of her car, and
curled up on the floor. After a while I heard her get in
and slam the door. She started the motor. I held my
breath. I didn't breathe. We began to move. We were
moving. I felt the vibration and heat of the motor
through the floor. My foot fell asleep. We drove and
drove for such a long time I had to go to the bathroom.
I was afraid I'd wet my pants. I wet my pants.

She didn't find me until she stopped at a gas station
and the man pumping gas asked her if the kid on the

floor in the back was sick. She wheeled around and hollered, My God what are you doing here! She was really upset. She was really mad. She yanked me out, put me in front, turned the car around and drove me home in my wet pants. She was so mad she wouldn't talk—just yelled that I ruined everything. I didn't care. I was glad I ruined everything. I was hungry and thirsty but she wouldn't stop—not even for a soda. But I didn't care about that, either. I was going home in the front seat with my mom.

But the Depression was waiting like a mean-eyed snake and when it hit, my mother had to put away her sparkling dresses and dancing shoes and stay home with Kenny and me. Still, everyone else was broke too; even men, even husbands and fathers, even the guiltless. The entire country had been on a binge, drunk on money and bootleg booze and the fantasy that it would never end and for once she was part of the mainstream, living not in orphanhood or gangsterhood or flapperhood but merely as one of millions who had lost everything and was suffering from a hangover of excess. And I had my mom back. The Great Depression had saved me. I was part of something now, a family, a community, a country.

We set up housekeeping. Sort of. Her raging claustrophobia kept us in constant motion. After the barred windows of the orphanage, after never being allowed outside the compound, movement anywhere—to the park, to the road, to another apartment or a different job or a new man—cheered her for a while. Unmoored, she moved us from apartment to apartment, often suffering with one of her asthma attacks, as unaware of her impulses as a feather in the wind. The moving van would take us to "better" rooms, a brighter future.

But when we arrived at the new apartment all we found was a place and a life just like the one we had left behind. It was as if the more she tried to escape the past, the more it confronted her, and then we were off again, running in place again. Each new apartment seemed as forlorn and hopeless as the last, smelling of cigarette smoke from a previous tenant's habit, or the fresh paint my mother had managed to negotiate with the landlord, or cooking smells, thick as wet wool; sausage, garlic, cabbage, that made my stomach turn with nausea and envy. Our window view was always the same, too, as if we had brought along the brick wall facing us from our last place. Inside, the rooms were shadowy, or seemed to be, as if meant just for sleeping or death.

The moving vans and packing boxes were as familiar to me as my mother's face. And so were her books. Every time we moved, her books were the first thing she unpacked—before the dishes or coffee pot, or ironing board (which was not taken down until the next move). Even before making up the beds. She went about her unpacking cheerfully, humming, fondling her books. Moving always put her in a good mood, as if the mere act of packing and unpacking would change her destiny.

She always kept her books nearby, like a lover. I stared at the dogeared volumes and held them because she loved them so much. *Das Kapital* by Karl Marx, Faulkner's *The Sound and the Fury,* and I remember two by Kafka—*The Castle* and *The Trial.* There was a play by Eugene O'Neill—I don't remember the name, but I do recall *Goodbye to All That* by Robert Graves, open on her nightstand—probably because even then I liked its lovely elegiac title and the smooth feel of the cover.

After my daddy died we settled into an apartment on Euclid Heights Boulevard. There were many rooms and a huge kitchen and an endlessly long hall that disappeared into the mysteries of my mother's bedroom.

"Smoke!" my mother screamed.

I was two and a half years old and the next thing I remember is being on the street in the bitter cold night. The building burned to the ground and since this was our first home after the murders, my mother could be forgiven if she wondered what evil forces were out there still knocking her around. Neighbors took us in. It was warm inside. I was fed milk and cookies. Kenny tells me that Uncle Marvin came and got us.

After the fire we moved to the Hotel Sovereign, then to successive apartments on Lakeview, Meadowbrook, Chapman. We lived on Lenox Road the time I got scarlet fever, and Hampshire where the landlady's fat son jumped me.

Then my mother sent me to live with Aunt Jane as a paying border while she went off to a hotel. I had to take two streetcars to get to school that bitter cold winter, and my cousin, a year older than I, wasn't thrilled with my presence. Too angry to feel my anger, I didn't tell my mother I wouldn't go. I didn't say: "Why are you doing this?" She volunteered a reason, something vague, but I didn't listen. I didn't hear it.

I was afraid she was having sex in a hotel—probably with someone married, probably Jack O'Brian, one of the engineers where she worked. The few times he had dinner with the three of us at the deli, she looked at him a way she never looked at me. Although he tried to be nice, putting on an Irish brogue and telling jokes, making my mother laugh, I hated him. I wanted him to go away. I knew with a child's canny instinct that he was married. Why else didn't he come over? Or take my mother out on a proper date like Milt Strauss? Why did she whisper into the phone every time he called and then get ready to go out? Her excitement getting dressed and the way she looked and smelled when she came home—a little mussed, a little sweaty, kind of lit up— worried me. It scared me.

What was having sex, exactly? What were she and Jack doing? In the movies the couple kiss and go into the bedroom. But then they shut the door. My best friend Phyllis said the man gets on top of the woman and pushes his seed with his thing into where she pees. Did Jack O'Brian push his seed into my mother? Did he hurt her? The next time he calls I'm going to hang up. The next time he calls I'll hide her car keys so she can't go out. I don't want him to get on top of my mother so she can hardly breathe. My daddy in heaven could stop all this stuff, this sex. He could make her stink. He could make Jack O'Brian get killed in a car wreck. He could do anything because he's a king and he's coming back to us.

"When I grow up and have a daughter I'm going to stay home," I told her.

She looked at me, amused. "Oh? And what if you can't? What if you're alone so you have to go out to have friends?"

"I won't be all alone," I said. "I'll have a real husband to stay home with." (Years later, stuck in misery with a real husband, I longed for my mother's life.)

Aunt Jane was cold and bossy and I didn't like her. I didn't like that my mother had to pay for my staying there, either, and my cousin had a mean streak a mile wide. We carried my two suitcases inside, my mother helped me unpack, and then she was gone. Gone. Her absence echoed in the apartment, reverberating in my ears. I felt defenseless, disposed of. Discarded.

That night I dream I'm in a hotel corridor, sitting on the floor, my back to the wall. I listen to the elevator doors open and close. I listen to my own heart pulse in my ears. I am waiting for my mother to come out of the room. The door finally opens but it is not my mother. It is someone else, a strange woman in a black veiled hat, and I weep in relief and disappointment. She doesn't see

41

me because I am invisible to everyone but my mother. I look up and down the long dark corridor trying to figure out which door she is behind. Then Jack O'Brian comes out of a room. He is smiling. I get up and run away.

Aunt Jane's apartment had carpeting and heavy furniture and regular meals. I tried to focus on the luxury of having a bedroom all to myself. And the nice hot sit-down dinners she served. I sat at the table with my cousin and the other boarders, a couple who had the big bedroom off the living room. But I didn't like them, either.

I missed my mother. I missed our screwed-up life. I missed the moving vans and packing boxes and the familiar ratty books that followed us from place to place. I missed my brother and the little white cartons of chop suey that my mother picked up on her way home from work, and our last apartment and the one before that. And I missed my father. Not the king in the sky of my fantasies—what I longed for was a flesh and blood dad—the kind that everyone else seemed to have, the kind that would get me out of here. Furious, sad, I sobbed silently into my pillow into the night.

When my mother finally came back for me, she seemed so quiet and sad, I wondered if she and Jack broke up. Or if maybe he refused to leave his wife and marry her. I didn't think she was the one who fell out of love because of the way she lunged for the phone every time it rang and the way her eyes got wet when it wasn't Jack. Then I'd hear her cry in the bedroom, as if I wasn't there, worrying, as if only Jack O'Brian mattered in the world. I wished I could get her back to the time before Jack O'Brian, to the way she was before love or passion or whatever it was stole her away.

I think maybe my daddy fixed Jack O'Brian good. He made him love his wife. He made her more beautiful than my mom.

I knew I would never figure out what really

happened. I didn't care. I had my mom back and we moved into a basement apartment on Overlook Drive with an iron-gridded window-view of wheels and feet. It was like existing below sea level. Then we lived in two different apartments on Cedar Road, six months and a block apart. Don't ask me why. The last place was on North Moreland, from where I got married. That was when my mother had to get all her teeth pulled even though she was only 44. When she got her new teeth she cried because they changed the shape of her mouth. With her teeth in she still looked good, but at night when she took them out her face got so crumpled I was afraid to look at her.

We moved so often that one neighborhood has melded into another in my memory; a kind of generic arrangement of Depression-era grocery stores, with their scrubbed wooden counters and penny candy in tall glass jars and good coffee smells and the long wand with its fascinating grippers the grocer used to pull cans down from the top shelf. I remember the drug store where I would sometimes spend the fifty cents my mother left me for dinner on a banana split. I'd sit on the stool at the soda fountain, eating slowly, trying to make my ice cream last long enough to get the attention of the handsome soda jerk who was always busy waiting on customers or flirting with some other older girl. Finally, I'd pay my check and go home.

But sometimes I'd eat at Hull Dobbs, a diner that had wonderful potatoes called butter fries. Often I'd see Patsy Rose there, who was a year or two older, and alone, too.

"Poor Patsy," my mother said. "Her mother sends her to eat alone at Hull Dobbs."

"But I was there, too! On the next stool!" I cried.

"Listen, Patsy's mother plays bridge. I have to go to work," she said proudly, as if she'd just been anointed Mother of the Year.

There was a deli on the corner where my mother and I would eat sometimes, also a dark shoe repair shop that smelled of leather, whose owner had blackened fingernails and a dark, glowering face when he turned from his machines to wait on you. There was a library within walking distance and, next to the shoemaker's, a Woolworths from which I stole, with a pounding heart, an all-day sucker decorated with a face. The bar in the neighborhood had a mysterious, darkened, faintly dangerous facade that speeded up my heart as I walked past, street smart enough to carefully avoid eye contact with the men sitting inside on stools or coming out unsteadily, blinking in the light.

I passed a mother pushing her baby in a stroller; a man in a coat and fedora with a newspaper tucked under his arm; a couple holding hands; a guy in overalls. Standing at the traffic light, they seemed to be connected horizontally to each other and vertically to sturdy roots, and who knows? maybe upwards to God. Standing outside their magic grid waiting for the light to change I imagined the fortified linkages of their lives, while I had nothing but the time and space to drift around like smoke, unconnected, being only who I was.

The first thing I did when I got home from school was call my mother at work. I loved her office telephone voice. She sounded like a real mom then, performing the role, I now know, for Jack O'Brian and her other office mates. Her telephone voice was different; calm, motherly. She asked about school, she laughed often, her laughter musical, thrilling me. She told me to meet her at the corner deli after work, or to come downtown on the streetcar to her office and we'd go to Mills Cafeteria. But later, at home, all that professional motherhood and cheerfulness and interest in me slipped away like a second skin. Turning inward she wilted in front of my eyes; I watched her alive downtown face change into something as listless and deadened as a wounded animal's in the road. And I was alone again.

I heard the voices of our next-door neighbors, their comings and goings, their radio: Jack Benny, Fred Allen, Amos 'n Andy. As the smell of meat loaf wafted out into the hall, I pictured their tidy rooms and busy, fragrant kitchen. Ours was bare, as if we were just passing through. Which I guess we were.

Four

"ARENT YOU THAT Rosen girl?" Mary Ann's mother said. Mary Ann Halloway was my new best friend in second grade and we were sitting in her kitchen drinking milk and eating coconut cookies. The cookies were delicious and something nice-smelling was cooking away on the stove. It was Saturday afternoon and her father was there, too. "The one whose father got murdered?"

"No," I said, chewing. "My daddy died of pneumonia."

"It was about five years ago," she went on, "some kind of bootlegging business. Let me think." She narrowed her eyes. "His name was Lester. Or Leon. No, wait a minute. Louis. That's it, Louis. Louis Rosen. And there was another one murdered—a brother, I think. It was in all the papers."

She turned to her husband. "I remember the name because it's Jewish. Most of those people who go around killing each other are Italian, but this was a Jew." She looked at me, got hold of her husband's hand, and pulled herself back as if I had the measles or something.

The coconut cookies on my stomach were suddenly on the way up. I stood, knocking over my milk. "I have to go home now."

"Yes, run along," Mrs. Halloway said, handing me my coat.

I got out of there just in time to throw up on Mrs. Halloway's azaleas.

I was not invited there again.

Which was OK by me. Mrs. Halloway made me mad; she made my heart bang. I wouldn't want her to be my mother even if all she did was make coconut cookies. Even if I could eat a million coconut cookies. People who were bootleggers and Jews sounded bad coming out of her mouth. But I had no idea what bootleggers did. Or Jews, either, for that matter. My mother's life had hardly turned her into a believer, and she didn't send me to Sunday school, a foreign destination reserved for other kids. All I understood about being Jewish was that our family didn't go to church. But we didn't go to temple, either.

I started to run home, but my feet seemed stuck as if I were running in place in a dream. I had believed Mrs. Halloway when she said the murdered Louis Rosen in the newspapers was my daddy, and I felt a wave of disloyalty to my mother that made my throat hurt; and in the next instant a shiver of pride that my daddy had done something so exciting and daring it was in the newspapers that he got killed.

But I felt ashamed, too, and I needed to talk to someone. When I got home, Kenny was out somewhere and my mother wasn't home from work yet, so I went back outside. It was almost six and the other kids had been called in to dinner. I played jacks by myself on the apartment stoop for a while and then hopscotch on the sidewalk. Then I discovered a nickel in my pocket and decided to walk over to Peterson's Drug Store for some candy. I liked it in there. Mr. Peterson always gave me a licorice stick when I bought a candy bar and let me hang around eating my candy and reading comics. Looking back, I think he felt sorry for me, but I liked my wanderings; it helped ease my loneliness. It comforted and consoled me. It made me feel free. It took my mind off home.

I went outside with my licorice stick and sat down on the curb. Mr. Peterson was nice but he was always busy unpacking boxes or waiting on customers and I needed someone to talk to. I needed to talk to my daddy. I shut my eyes tight and took a deep breath. Then I put my hands together like people do when they pray and looked up at the sky. Daddy? Are you up there? Can you hear me? See, other kids have real dads to talk to about stuff, but you're in a place I can't see. So I have to ask. Here's what I want to know. You heard what Mrs. Halloway said. So is it true? I think I know you aren't a king with pneumonia, but are you a Jew bootlegger who got murdered? If you can hear me send something through the air. Make your hanky fall in front of me on Euclid Avenue when I'm walking. Okay?

I got up and walked home on Euclid Avenue watching for my daddy's hanky but it didn't come down, so I guessed he was too busy or something. And by the time I got home that night Mrs. Halloway and Jew bootleggers had slipped back into the secrets and out of my mind.

I would often drift around like that, the days without beginnings or ends, skipping school with the sun on my back like a warm hand, riding streetcars, reading in the library, staying too long in a friend's house until the mother sent me home. My friends were fascinated and envious of my roaming ways and their parents wide-eyed with concern. But as if surviving murder means you've used up your lifetime's share of danger, I felt safe. I wasn't, of course, but I thought I was. Walking home from the library at night under an umbrella of stars, or wandering in the park, I thought my father was watching out for me from heaven with his gun. I really did. He would never let anything bad happen to me because he was powerful and dangerous and he loved me. And although I had obscene proposals shouted (and whispered) to me, innocently made friends at the age of nine with a fifteen-year-old prostitute, observed mastur-bators in the park, and once on the streetcar (they didn't scare me because they seemed to be intent on the business at hand), I wasn't raped or murdered.

But just in case my daddy was distracted or busy doing something else up there in heaven, I was careful. I became my own parent. I crossed streets with the light, made no eye contact with strangers, watched out for stray dogs. I took a sweater along in the summer heat and mittens and a scarf on mild winter days. And for emergencies I carried a stone. I understood the violence in the air.

One day my friend Helene tagged along when I skipped school. She talked all through the movie and on the way home I had to snatch her back to the curb when she was almost run over. Another time she ate so much candy from Woolworths, she threw up in the Ladies. Walking home that day it turned cold and she shivered so hard I had to give her my sweater.

I got tired of taking care of Helene and wouldn't let her go with me again unless she let me ride her bike after school for a week. The only thing I really liked about her anyway was that she could walk backward without looking, which I found thrilling. One day after school she tagged along home with me because I had gone to her house so often to play with her doll house. But when we got to our apartment building I was too ashamed of our messy place to let her come upstairs. I told her that my brother had scarlet fever.

So we played jacks on our apartment stoop. Suddenly I burst into tears, surprising both of us. She called me a poor loser, but that wasn't it. I had just started to feel sad. I didn't know why. It was as if something bad had happened that I couldn't remember.

"Your nose is running," Helene said with great disgust.

I wiped the snot on my sleeve. Watching, she pretended to throw up.

Helene, like Nancy and Mary Ann and my other school friends, was chaperoned, supervised, fed milk and cookies. Taken to ballet lessons, piano lessons, Sunday School. Made to do homework, clean up their rooms, eat their vegetables. Their mothers said how was school; they asked if there was still a substitute teacher in geography and if they needed milk-money. They said don't you dare go out without your galoshes. They said a penny for your thoughts. I heard them. My mother never said those things to me or asked questions. It was as if I existed merely as her shadow or forgotten appendage.

I was the one with the curiosity. I wanted to know everything about my mother; what she whispered about on the telephone, where she went with her hat and earrings, what she talked about with her girlfriends, what she did on her dates. I wondered, worried, if she felt sad, if she would get one of her asthma attacks, if she was lonely. If she was afraid. Looking back I think worrying about her was easier than feeling my own sorrow and abandonment. And anger. Feeling her feelings was easier than feeling mine.

Sometimes I pretended she would come into my room after one of her dates and sit on my bed. "Babbie, I'm scared," she'd say.

"Why?"

"Well, coming home I thought I was getting an asthma attack, but now that I'm with you I'm feeling a lot better."

"Okay, Mom," I'd say. "Take a deep breath and count to ten. Then I want you to go into the bathroom and run the hot water and when the room fills with steam take ten more deep breaths. Okay? Meanwhile I'll get the vaporizer ready."

"Oh, Babbie, you always help me so much. Thank you, dear. I'm ready to go to bed now," she'd say, giving me a big hug. "Good night, honey."

We envied each other—my friends and I; they envied my freedom, I envied their aproned, hovering mothers, their sheltered, defended days. Walking home with Nancy from school one day I bopped her one on the head. She ran home bawling and then I felt like crying. Another time in the playground I put my foot out and tripped Alice McCoy while she was running a relay race. She went sliding on the gravel and the principal had to take her to the emergency room to get her bloody knee stitched up. I was kept after school to clean blackboards and erasers for three weeks after that.

The teacher called my mother to come in for a conference about my bad behavior and poor attendance. So she got herself up in an outfit from her high-flying flapper days and made a grand entrance into the classroom, causing a definite buzz. "Is that your *mother*?" my classmates whispered, pointing as she stood like a movie star in her veiled hat and gloves and the fur scarf with the mean little animal face draped over her shoulder.

That night when I asked her about the conference, she said, What do those stupid teachers know, and went back to her book.

But maybe my mother thought I would be all right wandering around alone out there; life was considered so safe no one locked their doors, and on hot nights in those days before air conditioning my mother and I would actually sleep in the park. We'd find an empty spot among the other families in makeshift beds, spread out newspapers, arrange our pillows and stretch out. It was like being at the beach except that instead of the blazing sun there was a dark sky and moon overhead and a few blessed random breezes. There would be the aroma of something sweet, like a honeysuckle vine growing somewhere, or someone's perfume, and you'd hear the murmur of voices and a radio playing softly. One night the couple next to us had their radio turned on to "Fibber McGee and Molly"—a program my mother hated. After lying with her eyes closed and mouth clenched she suddenly reared up as if stung by a bee and told them to shut that damn thing off. Which they promptly did. My mother had that effect on people.

Actually, the only time I was accosted was at home. My mother had rented rooms in some woman's apartment on Hampshire Road that smelled of the old orange cat that took possession of the only comfortable chair in the living room. The landlady had tight red curls, a double chin, and wore dangling earrings and those flowing muumuus that fat people dress in. Her son, Frankie, gave me the creeps. He was fifteen and I'd catch him spying on me while he lurked around the apartment. The rooms were small and dark; they had a musty smell and I hated it there.

I am home alone with a cold. Frankie suddenly grabs me from nowhere, shoves me down on the floor, gets on top of me in his clothes, holds my arms down and starts pumping away. I press my legs together from my ankles to my thighs. I stop breathing. My middle region turns to water. Fear shuts me down so I feel nothing—not even his hard-on. My head, my entire body has stopped itself and I cannot move or get out from under this heavy, gasping mass of flesh. I want to scream but no one is home, and anyway, if I'm found here under him they'll think it's my fault, that I'd asked for it, like people say about girls who get into trouble. His breathing is wet and fast. Tears stream down my face, and my dress is wet with something else. I think he peed in his pants. I feel the wind slammed out of me and then a sudden awareness of the disarray and menace of the world.

When he lets go of my arms, I sock him, knocking

off his eyeglasses. He rolls off me and starts feeling around like a blind person. I jump up and stomp on his spectacles so hard you can hear the crunch as they break into a million splinters.

"Hey! Whad'ja do! I can't see!" he hollers.

"I'm telling!" I scream, as he feels his way down the hall. I am so mad I am crying. And when I finally see what had made my dress wet I kick on his door until my foot hurts so bad I think it's broken. I go to my room, change my clothes, and worry that I'll get pregnant when I start menstruating. I am ten years old.

I knew I hadn't invited this—I really hated that boy on sight. But maybe I had. Sex scared me but it fascinated me, too, and maybe that boy read my mind when I thought about what men and women did together.

The only information I had about sex was what my friend, Gloria, had told me. She was sixteen. Gloria and I went to the movies together on Friday nights after she got off work at Grant's Cafe. She had pulled-back mousy brown hair, pale skin, and a dancer's nervy carriage that would have pleased even Miss Brumelmeyer, my gym teacher who socked me on the back when I slouched, shouting *posture*!!

One night as the usher showed Gloria and me to seats in the dark theater, her knees suddenly buckled under her and she fainted dead away. The usher picked her up off the floor and carried her back up the aisle. Alarmed, I followed him to an office in the back. It smelled of stale popcorn. He laid her down on the couch.

"Water," Gloria whispered.

As soon as the usher ran out, she sat up and winked at me. By the time I had recovered enough from amazement to speak, he had dashed back in with a paper cup of water and Gloria had collapsed back on the couch. When he held the cup to her lips she stroked his hand with her fingertips.

"Babbie, go on home," she said in her weak voice. "Danny here will take care of me."

But I had already got the picture and I don't mean the one on the movie screen. It didn't occur to me until I found myself outside that I could have sat down and watched the movie. It was one of those Myrna Loy, William Powell mysteries. The one after *The Thin Man*.

After that night she told me all about her sex life. How she brought Johnny Spango home, who was a regular at the cafe. Speaking with pride as if she were powerful, she said they had sex on the couch while her mother was passed out in the bedroom, and that Danny, the usher, had simply unbuttoned his fly and got on top of her. On Saturdays after the restaurant closed, she said she had sex with her boss, Mr. Grant, sitting on the edge of the sink in the basement bathroom with her uniform pulled up and her legs on his shoulders. She dismissed Oscar, the cook, as being too grumpy. "So far," she added, grinning. "Although he could be one of those queers." She never wore panties, she told me, although as a matter of pride, she never took her clothes off, nor would she permit her boyfriends to do more than unbutton their pants.

All this sex talk scared and excited me. It made me want to cover my ears. My mother never brought a man home like Gloria did, or even mentioned sex. All I really knew about sex was that it was how you got pregnant.

"Aren't you afraid you'll get a baby?" I asked her.

"I guess I'm just a damn fool," Gloria said, proudly.

When she told me that she was through with Danny the usher I agreed to go to the movies with her the following Friday night. "Some men are pests afterwards," she said, "but Danny'll be easy to get rid of."

She had me come to the restaurant to wait for her. I sat at the counter drinking the cherry coke she gave me, and watched her dash around waiting on customers in her crisp pink uniform and white nurse's shoes. She was all business. She didn't even flirt. "You don't mix business with pleasure," she told me as we walked to the theater. "If I pick someone it's my choice," she said, "not theirs." Going into the theater, she was true to her word, turning her back on Danny's shiny-eyed greeting.

Walking home after the movie, Gloria told me about her father. "My daddy was a minister. He told me I was going straight to hell. I ran away."

"You ran away? Where to?"

"He wanted to fuck me," she said, cracking her gum.

"Where was your mother?"

"He said I was wild but all I was doing was riding around with boys drinking beer. I hadn't even screwed anyone yet and I sure as hell wasn't about to start with my own daddy."

After Frankie jumped me I didn't want to see Gloria any more and I didn't answer the doorbell when she came over. I wanted to get out of that apartment, away from Frankie, away from Gloria. I wanted to be ten years old.

If I was ten the right way I would have a white room, like cream. There are eight pillows on my bed. Sometimes I put them in a circle and sit in the middle with my doll. I read her from my book of Grimms Fairy Tales. My daddy always brings me a teddy bear when he comes home from a business trip and they're all lined up on the shelves with my dolls. There's a window seat with a cushion on it like Helene has in her room, only mine is bigger and has a view of a real apple tree. My mom buys me too many dresses so the closet's a mess and I have a new record player like I saw in Jayson's Hardware.

When my mother came home from work I raised hell until she promised we would move. And the next morning at breakfast with Frankie, his mother and my mother, I asked him sweetly what had happened to his glasses and watched his stupid fat face get red.

Years later I wondered why Gloria wanted to hang out with a ten-year-old. Or why my mother let me spend Friday nights with a sixteen-year-old waitress. Had she handed me over to Gloria for my sex education? Was that it? After all, the only information she ever gave me was in the two library books about the birds and bees she silently handed over before dashing from the room. They had nothing in them about menstruation because when I got my first period while in the hospital with scarlet fever, a nurse tossed a Kotex and strips of gauze on my bed and kept on walking. In my embarrassing, appalling ignorance, I didn't know what to do with them. As the sheet grew sticky and wet under me, another nurse finally put me out of my misery and strapped and swaddled me in.

"The scarlet fever brought it on," my mother said when I told her, as if menstruation was a side effect of disease. I got no beaming lecture on the body becoming ready for the joys of motherhood. For sex and love. Or a brisk reminder of the dangers of fooling around. There was no acknowledgement of a feminine milestone, or sentimental watershed. Not that I expected it. But I did.

But my mother was raised in a Victorian orphanage and would actually color and leave the room if anyone told a risque joke or uttered a four-letter word. Still, in her usual confusing tangle of contradictions, I saw how sexy, shined up and flirtatious she was around Milt and Jack, and later, even *my* dates.

"Well, hello!" she would sing, coming into the living room, batting her eyes like one of those silent movie stars. Sometimes she would stand in the doorway, smiling with her head raised as if someone was taking her picture. If we were playing records and she was in a good mood she'd actually start dancing, swishing her skirt from side to side like a Busby

Berkeley girl. I couldn't look at her, but my dates raved. They had never seen a mother like her.

After Frankie, I felt safer on the streets than in our apartment and kept to my wandering ways. But I hurried past the houses on the tree-shaded streets lest I start howling with envy over the families gathered behind the forbidden yellow glow of their windows.

I went to the library. The books on the shelves were my friends, their stories waiting to take me out of my life. I loved the long shiny tables. I loved pulling down one of the lined-up encyclopedias and the way its weighty pages would transform my confusing, baffling world into the wonder of an orderly alphabetized universe. The walls of soft-colored volumes were windows of stained glass, and the reverent hush of the people around me, worshippers in the church I never got into. Miss Allen, the librarian, was my mother handing me a book she thought I'd like, or telling me to lower my voice, or that my books were overdue, or to go home because the library was closing. I liked Miss Allen. I loved Miss Allen. When she put on her coat and turned out the lights I wanted to go with her.

Walking home one night, a man pulled his car over to the curb and said I'll put my tongue in your hole. Shaking, I ran in terror to a nearby apartment foyer, rang all the bells, shut my eyes and crouched in the corner. Two or three buzzers sounded in response, but half paralyzed with fear I didn't get to the doorknob in time and it locked again. After a while I peered through the glass door. His car was gone. I came out with shaking knees and went home.

My mother was there but I kept quiet about the tongue man, the way I had about Frankie. The thing about my mother was you never knew what she would do when you told her something—collapse into hysteria (as she did when a policeman caught Kenny joy-riding in her car), or hardly look up from her newspaper (like the time I confessed to skipping school). Or maybe say it was my fault and send me away to that vague, terrible place she came from. Orphanages were supposed to stay safely in stories and comic strips, they weren't meant to lurk menacingly on the edges of your own life as history, as threat. But in our family "orphanage" had the sad wail of reality, and if you don't know if your mother will collapse, ignore you, or send you away when you tell her something, you tend to keep your mouth shut around the house. I didn't mind. My mother may have been mercurial, but my phantom father watched over me and was as constant and steady as the sky.

But he couldn't seem to keep me from getting lost. He was busy. In my wanderings around town I lost my way so often it was as if my secret daddy had blindfolded me, twirled me round and round in a grotesque pin-the-tail-on-the-donkey game, and then turned me loose in the world. To this day maps depress me and I am defeated by addresses; dogs and small children have a far better sense of direction and place-memory than I do, finding their way with ease while I wind up on the other side of town. Leaving a hotel room I walk the wrong way in the corridor, and the diabolically slanted streets in Washington, DC, that angle crazily off circles have brought me to tears behind the wheel and into dangerous neighborhoods. I stick carefully to the interstates with their signs, exit numbers and arrows, and the labeled streets of geometric grids, as if such landmarks could steer me away from my father's killing streets.

Five

I'M SITTING IN Dr. Herman's waiting room, still smarting from yesterday's session. I didn't want to come back. But strung tight, thinking of how I stumble through my days trying to be careful, trying to anticipate Nate's next verbal assault, trying to ward it off when it comes, too guilty, too confused, too reduced, to know how, my youth spent in an old woman's caution, I sit here wishing I am somewhere else.

His office door opens. "Good afternoon," he says. "Come in."

Although he is standing quietly in a good suit, although he is pale-skinned and polite, I feel the primitive seduction of an African witch doctor. I walk into the room as if hypnotized and lie down obediently on the couch. Dr. Herman positions himself in his chair behind me. I hear him breathe. I stretch out my legs and put my hands under my head. A truck rumbles by.

He waits.

I clear my throat. "Okay, so I don't defend myself. I told you that. But I explained yesterday. I told you it's my fault, that I'm always doing something wrong."

Silence.

"You think I'm cowering for my keep or something. Like I'm some kind of stray. Don't you."

"Perhaps it's what you think about yourself."

I'm getting mad. "Listen here," I say. " I have two maids, a big house. A yacht. 55 feet. A 55-foot yacht named the *Babette*. We've just come back from Europe. We belong to a country club."

Silence.

I want to hit him.

"Why don't you say something!" I cry.

"I can say that your anger means we're on to something important here," he says.

I hear the hum of the drill in the dentist's office next door. Root canal is a piece of cake compared to this. Root canal doesn't scare me as much as this silent witch doctor sitting behind me who I can't even see. This is impossible. Maybe the guy getting his teeth drilled will change places with me. I'll knock on the wall and signal in Morse code. You dig into your marriage and I'll get my teeth drilled. My marriage for your teeth. Except I don't know Morse code. It strikes me funny that if I knew Morse code I could change places with some guy getting his teeth drilled. I laugh. I wonder if I'm going crazy. Well, then, I'm in the right place. I laugh again.

"What's funny?"

"I'd rather have root canal," I tell him.

Silence.

"This lady sits down in the dentist's chair," I say. "I'd rather have a baby, she remarks. Make up your mind, the dentist tells her, I have to adjust the chair."

No answer.

"That was a joke," I say.

"I know that was a joke."

"Then why aren't you laughing?"

"Because you have better things to do in here than tell jokes. To paraphrase your joke—make up your mind if you'd rather fix your tooth or fix your life."

"My life is okay. There's nothing wrong with my life. I just told you."

"Oh? Then what are you doing here?"

"That's what I'd like to know," I say.

"I think you already do know."

I am crying. All I seem able to do in here is cry. I turn over and sob into the leather couch. I sit up and hold my head in my hands and bawl. I don't know what to do with myself. Dr. Herman hands me some Kleenex. I grab his hand. He lets me. I hang on. My face is soaked and my nose is running. This is too much. Too much. I can't do this. I cry until Dr. Herman gently pulls his hand away and says, "Our time's up."

Still, I come back Mondays through Fridays at five o'clock, lie down on the couch and ramble on for 50 minutes, while Dr. Herman sits behind me without uttering a word. If I ask him what he thinks about a dream I'd had, he asks me what I think he thinks. When I ask if he is married or has children, his answer is a maddening silence. He infuriates me. He drives me crazy. I want to scream or storm out of there or hit him. But I remain as dutiful an analysand as I am a daughter, wife and mother, and most of that first year lie on the couch wondering what the hell I'm doing there.

Sometimes I sob repressed tears into his silence. Once I fell asleep. But I am getting the idea. He keeps himself a blank screen on which to project my fantasies, dreams and transferences, and then helps me interpret and understand them. It forces me to look inward—there is no other place I can go in this dim, quiet room. This couch and this mute man are my last hope.

He refuses to give me advice. I ask him if he would tell me not to do something dangerous, like running away, because I fantasize about being one of those runaway wives. I go to a motel, where everything is competent, efficient, in order and ordinary; a place where you can't start screaming. There is a bed, a dresser, the smells of stale perfume and stale sex, a bathroom, the toilet with its reassuring paper strip. A blue bedspread in a flowered design with matching draperies you can close with a pull on a string. A painting on the wall: gondolas in Venice. A television set. Ed Sullivan. Milton Berle. I sit on the bed and watch the afternoon game shows in a place where everything is predictable, comprehensible, calm, and as detached as I feel or am trying to feel. In a room like that maybe Nate will cease to matter; maybe I won't care so much; maybe I won't feel so humiliated, so disappointed in myself.

But Dr. Herman doesn't have to tell me not to run away. I know I won't do it. You can't run away with three children to a motel room that you have no money to pay for, with a husband who will find you anyway. Besides, I don't want to sit on a bed watching game shows. I want to be home with my children, the kind of woman who doesn't fill her husband with disdain.

So I ride the analyst's couch back into my childhood and see the murders and my unparented childhood from the safety of that room, as if Dr. Herman is holding my hand as I go back, back, into the abyss. I weep for the first time at all my losses and begin to find a place within myself that can accommodate my history without having it reach up and direct my life.

Every couple of weeks Dr. Herman interprets my actions and choices, dreams, and ramblings. Then he clams up again. Although I come to some of the truths reluctantly and painfully, being listened to and under-stood, and then beginning to understand myself, is such an exquisite relief that it keeps me coming back.

Six

DO CRIMINALS RUN in families like blue eyes and multiple sclerosis? I worried about that because in order for gangsters to exist there had to be gangsters' parents and grandparents and all manner of forebears. All Kenny had to do was stay out late and my mother would worry that he was turning into his father, on his way to a violent death. Sometimes their arguments would turn into a free-for-all, with my grandma Anna jumping in, cursing in Yiddish, sucking on her false teeth, hollering louder than anyone. (Years later I realized that the only Yiddish words I knew were unrepeatable in polite society.) She had moved in with us because my mother supported her and there wasn't enough money for a place of her own.

Grandma criticized everything my mother said, wore, and did. Kenny was going straight to hell gallivanting around with his wild ways, I was neglected, I was too skinny, I had never learned discipline or chores. If a man called my mother on the phone when she was out, she didn't give her the message, and if my mother was home and answered the telephone, Gram would run the vacuum cleaner around her feet so she couldn't hear what the caller was saying. Then, in between her rantings she sat on the couch in such utter silence it was as if she was carved in stone, coming to life only for a good fight.

She hollered about what the world had done to her. She battled about money or the lack thereof, or what someone did or didn't do, or said or didn't say, grinning in her rage, the smile on her face scarier than her hollering. My mother would yell back, or cry, or slam out the door. Sometimes she got an asthma attack. Her asthma was such an ongoing fact of our family life that in utter familiarity Kenny and I would hear her moist, rattling breathing, see her face drain of color, dash for the respirator, and watch in helpless terror as she bent over it with desperate gasps.

I hung around the fights—my family was crazy but it was mine. I tried to get Gram to sit down at her place on the couch or push Kenny out the door. Eleven years old, I was a one person UN, a self-appointed minister of peace. If Amy, who lived a floor below, asked me at school the next day about the room-rocking commotion, it took no effort on my part to just shrug. If nothing can be done people stay calm—they pile furniture on the roof in a flood, stand in their pajamas in the driveway watching their house burn down, ride in an ambulance holding a stricken child's hand. Or maybe those fights made me feel, in my ridiculous calm, reassured of my own sanity.

Gram's coming made us all worse. One night a policeman brought Kenny home after catching him driving around in our mother's car. My mother had more of her temper fits, I rarely showed up in class and came home later than ever. Kenny began tormenting me, chasing me with the bugs I hated, making a monster face at night in my room with a flashlight under his chin, starting water fights, food fights, locking me out, pulling my hair, doing anything he could think of to torture me.

When they weren't fighting, Kenny and my mother discussed politics and books and world events, arguing their positions like an old married couple. She depended on him for advice and attention, took his arm while walking and expected him to help her with her coat, listen to her complaints, open doors and light her cigarettes as if he were actually her husband or boyfriend. "Cigarootte me, toot," she would say, and then try to puff like Bette Davis in the movies. Going to the deli, her arm linked with his, wearing her veiled hat, she could have been 25—she looked so young that Kenny, tall for his age and worried-looking, was sometimes taken for her husband. Which delighted my mother and turned Kenny sullen. He had the unfortunate role of adult male surrogate. My role was to keep the peace, not upset my mother and secretly watch out for her. Hers was to go to work, get paid, come home and not kill herself.

My mother and I had somehow reversed our roles, with me worrying about her health, her dates, her job, *her*. Even at eleven I knew she was hanging on by her fingernails. Even at eleven I knew that Gram had the resilience of the truly mean and disconnected, and Kenny the raw arrogance and strength of a fifteen-year-old male big for his age. It was my raging, crying, hysterical mother who was vulnerable and over-whelmed, who already at the age of 35 had had several lifetimes of misfortune dumped on her from a lopsided God who couldn't seem to get his distribution of bad/good luck right among his helpless subjects. You'd think her sad, orphaned childhood would have tough-ened her for the unlucky vicissitudes of life, but it was the opposite, as if those heartbreaking years had stripped her skin away, her protective covering, leaving her with exposed nerve ends.

There was no one, as far as I could tell, whom she could talk to about what happened to my daddy, about her loss of hope and love. Her anger. Her loneliness and terror. The hysteria that lay just back of her throat. Her secrets or her shame kept her mute. What she had longed for and lost, or never had, was no more or less than anyone else in the world would want, and she tried to get it, or some of it, or a little of it, from a boyfriend or two, a married lover, an office friend. She was on the edge with no hand outstretched in love or fear or guilt to pull her back.

I thought it would have to be me.

In the bedroom I look down at my skinny body, then I stare at my small self in the mirror. I have to do something. I have to get bigger. And tougher. I stand on my toes and stretch my arms high to get tall. I puff up my chest with big breaths and practice punching the air with my fists.

Then I close my eyes and pretend to march into the living room where my mother is lying on the couch with her arms dangling over the side.

Mom, it's time to get up, I say.

She raises her head and looks at me in surprise but she doesn't move. Just grunts something.

Now, now, this won't do, I say. You're okay, we're all okay. You've got to rise and shine! You've got to get going! I lean against the wall and fold my arms. Come on now, get up and wash your face. Your hair's a mess and your dress is wrinkled. And look at this room! I'll be back in fifteen minutes and I want you up and dressed, and this room cleaned up. Okay, dear? You'll feel better if you mind me. See you in fifteen minutes!

When Gram made me a costume of purple cheesecloth on her sewing machine like a regular normal grandmother I was more thrilled with my flowing robes than my starring role in the Christmas play, or with the beautiful doll as the baby Jesus they gave me to hold. (Being chosen as Mary surprised and amused everyone because I was the only Jewish kid in the school.)

Walking home one day after rehearsal I was concentrating on avoiding the cracks in the sidewalk, because everyone knew *Step on a crack you'll break your mother's back*. I wasn't sure just how that worked, but just in case, I watched, I was careful. We had enough trouble.

Suddenly I felt a snowball sting the back of my neck. Turning around I got hit in the face with another one.

"You cut that out!" I screamed at Ralphie Ryan and Kevin Webster.

"Dirty Jew! Christ killer!" they hollered, pelting me with a barrage of snowballs.

"I'm telling! I'll telling my big brother on you!" I yelled.

Crying, I ran as fast as I could, feeling the sting of snowballs pelt my back. By the time I got home I was covered with snow.

Kenny was on his way out. "Kenny! Wait!" I screamed. "Wait! Ralphie and Kevin! They hit me with snowballs! They called me dirty Jew! I said you'd get them!"

"What'd you tell 'em that for? Are you crazy?" And he slammed out of the apartment.

I went in the bedroom to change my wet clothes. I was crying. Kenny had left me behind. He was in his teens. He didn't want to be my big brother or my father or our mother's husband any more.

Although Gram complained constantly that she had too much work cooking and cleaning for the three of us, and that (although she seemed ancient to me) we'd send her to an early grave, she didn't actually die for decades, not until I was grown. When the doctor told my mother that it was syphilis that killed her, my mother actually fainted dead away. But it also helped us understand that the disease had already penetrated her brain when she lived with us. At her funeral we all pretended we were a normal family burying a beloved mother and grandmother. But I didn't mourn. She had made my mother cry too much.

I retreated to the movies. Presenting my dime to the lady

in the box office, I clutched my ticket, walked a half dozen steps and was enclosed in the dark; a few more steps and my eyes could make out the seats. Finding my way down the aisle to the front row, I was ready to be taken into other lives.

The strangers silhouetted around me were like silent comrades and the plots of films with titles like *Stage Mother* and *For Heaven's Sake* made more sense to me than the furies swirling around at home. Event followed event in a semblance of order. Loose ends were tied up; problems resolved; virtue rewarded. You knew who the bad guys were (Boris Karloff, Charles Laughton). The women were beautiful (Constance Cummings, Marion Davies); lovers were reunited; danger and all obstacles to happiness overcome. The heroes (Ronald Colman, Franchot Tone) were saved, the endings happy. I loved the newsreels, too. The disembodied sonorous voice-over seemed to emanate from God himself in its omnipotent, awesome knowledge of all things from beauty contests to prize fights to the Kansas drought and the German elections.

For entire Saturday afternoons at the Cedar-Lee Theater I watched the same movie over and over. When James Cagney or Edward G. Robinson died at the end I knew that as long as I sat there he would return, his reincarnated, shimmering presence on the screen in front of me as unreal and as real as my father's. When Robert Young or Paul Muni disappeared after the last reel I knew he'd be back; I was sitting with my daddy and his gossamer, magical comrades; I was in their stories; they loved me and I was safe. I sat there until Kenny came and hauled me out, blinking in the light.

I could have told you the plot of every movie I had seen for the last six months, but once away from the theater's friendly darkness, once back in the bright glare of real life, I existed in a willed amnesia. I forgot homework and my books, lost my coat, sweater, mittens, money. My mother got upset but I just shrugged. I didn't mind. For all I knew my daddy's sleight of hand had whisked my sweater or coat away; they vanished as mysteriously as he had. "Don't ever have a baby," my mother warned me. "You'll forget and leave it on the streetcar." But feeling pleasantly hazy and insulated within my skin like that lovely dreamy numbness you get after the first rush from one of the martinis I later took up, I was drunk on my father's life after death, consumed into a pit of forbidden secrets, alone, neither rescued nor damned.

Once at my friend Martha's house I saw her father. He was sitting in the living room wearing an undershirt stretched over his big belly. He smelled of beer and sweat, and Martha and her mother seemed afraid of him. I didn't understand then all the importance everyone seemed to give to living, ordinary, mortal, powerless fathers who hollered and smelled and punished and took up space and were catered to and feared, while mine was flat-bellied and handsome and young and would never leave me to play golf or go bowling or to work or die of old age. He was dead so he was mine, all mine and always would be. He was brave and handsome and good and he loved me above all others.

Yet something was wrong. I couldn't seem to reach my daddy anymore. He even forgot to send me a hanky. Well, maybe he thinks I'm still two years old. Or maybe time's different where he is.

Or he could be too sick with pneumonia. I could take care of him! I clench my fists and shut my eyes trying to figure something out. But all I see is a silly old castle in a pink sky like a picture in a book for kids. And when I open my eyes again I see nothing but my mother's room with the door closed.

If he were here like other fathers, he'd give me the dog I long for to keep me company or the bike that will give me wings. (Years later I had a three-speed bike.

And a Dual Ghia—then just like Frank Sinatra's car—with my name engraved on a gold plate on the dashboard, and neither one could replace in my heart that Schwinn two-wheeler I never got.) Or a trip to an amusement park. Calm strong arms to pull me out of a nightmare. A lecture over a bad report card. My birthstone in a small box. Sundays at the beach watching that I don't go out too far. A backyard swing, a hug. Order in my days. I stared at a father and daughter holding hands in the park; a baby held by her dad fascinated me. Fathers and daughters seemed so commonplace to me, it was as if I alone was unworthy of such an ordinary arrangement, and feeling a dazzling and depthless loss, I pressed my nose against the window of families like Martha's and Helene's.

So maybe having a phantom father in the sky wasn't so great after all. Maybe a real dad who actually died in bed of respectable pneumonia was better. I needed to talk to my mother about which was which; I needed to know which one of us had made him up.

One morning I wrote down the questions I wanted to ask her:

> Did he really die of pneumonia?
> Did he get murdered?
> Was he bad?

The shop where my mother had sold dresses on commission had gone under and she had been teaching herself shorthand and bookkeeping from a pile of library books spread out on the kitchen table. Although her new office skills landed her a job in the Engineering Department of the City Hall, she was exhausted from cramming and so nervous about starting the next day, she hadn't been able to sleep for two nights.

Kenny remembers our mother as being frightened, and I remember her as being brave. I think we were both right. Fragile, lonely, asthmatic, often hysterical, frequently bewildered, it was as if she were watching for something or someone to rise up and provide her with information on how to proceed, on what to do next. But her ferocious pride kept us going during the Great Depression, she looked like a duchess in the bargain-basement dresses she wore on dates and to work, read Hardy and James and Wharton, and saw everything on Broadway from standing room ("when everyone gets up I sit down," she told me proudly). And no matter what, every single Saturday the radio filled our apartment with opera. Summers, she drove us 500 miles over unpaved roads to her sister's when few women drove alone around the block, and she could make a rude saleslady wish she were dead with her amazingly inventive insults. Standing at the level of her shoulder, I was embarrassed, but also secretly pleased, as if she were my surrogate mouthpiece expressing my anger at the world.

She was only five feet four but when she stood she seemed to tower over everyone, electrifying a room with her brilliance and charm. Words spilled from her mouth as if she had to relieve herself of her teeming brain, but she didn't know when or how to stop. People became restless; they looked away; they would leave if they could.

When Kenny and I were older we would sometimes imagine her in a different life—a senator or the first woman vice-president. A college professor lecturing in a perfect suit, her students frantically scribbling, trying to keep up with her racing mind. A lawyer arguing her case, pacing nervously in front of the jury. Not a doctor; she was too squeamish and on-edge to be a doctor. Rather one of those arrogant, grand Washington hostesses with the city's powerful A-list at her perfect table, everyone vying for invitations. She would have been a natural for that role because it is true that in spite of her humble beginnings she was a snob.

Or we could see her in another time: in a ballroom with flower-filled vases, Strauss waltzes and romantic secrets. Waving a flirtatious fan back and forth across her face against the summer heat. Seated at an elegant dinner table of candle-lit polished wood and gleaming silver, in a gown of mauve silk, jewels glittering at her ears and throat.

Given the miserable facts of her real life, these imaginings became a little silly, but Kenny and I would indulge in them every once in a while anyway. It made us feel better.

She had light-colored eyes and great bones, and when she was dressed up for a date in her high heels and jangling bracelets you couldn't help looking at her. On Sundays, though, hanging around the apartment in her robe and slippers she always looked washed-out and sort of gray. Then, going to work in the morning, she looked different again, putting me in mind of the Duchess of Windsor in the newsreels; she had the same aquiline nose, thin mouth, and crisp elegance.

But now I could see she was tired, stretched out on the couch, reading the Sunday papers. She was wearing her faded blue and white flowered housecoat with the front zipper. There was a blazing August sun beating against the window and she had put a bowl of ice cubes in front of our fan which was blowing a nice little breeze into the room. Outside the streets were quiet with Sunday morning.

She put the paper down when she saw me. "Did you do your homework?"

I looked at her. Every once in a while she acted like a regular normal mother. But it was just another role and it irritated me. Of course I didn't do my homework. I never did my homework. Which she knew full well.

Going to school and doing homework had nothing to do with me. Going to school and doing homework was for the mysterious families who lived inside regular houses and didn't harbor a secret like a madwoman in the attic.

I needed other lessons but I didn't know what they were.

"Where were you last night?" she asked.

She really was getting into it. "Around," I said.

"Really, Babbie, 8 o'clock is too late to be coming home."

I didn't know whether to laugh or cry. I had been coming home at 8 o'clock all my life.

I looked at the paper I had crumpled up in my fist with the written-down questions. But I lost my nerve. There was no way I could even mention murder. I needed to begin with something safer, slower. "Mom," I said, "how old was my daddy when he died?" She didn't look up but as I watched, little beads of perspiration broke out over her upper lip.

"Mom?" I said again.

"Oh, look!" she exclaimed in a girlish voice. "Halle's is having a sale on winter coats!" She turned the newspaper toward me. "Isn't that good-looking for $19.95?"

The concern about my mother that circulated within me like my blood turned into bile. I wanted to hit her. I wanted to grab the newspaper from her hands and tear it into shreds. I had to get out of there before I started crying.

The next time I brought it up she was in the kitchen putting away groceries. She was in her slip. My mother always took off her good clothes the minute she got home from work. Sometimes she forgot and left her hat on, but she always hung her dress up carefully, and even if dishes were piled up in the sink and you could write your name in the dust on the table, she always looked perfect when she went out.

"So, Mom," I said, "do we have a picture of my daddy anywhere around?"

Pain swept over her face. "I think I'll take a bath," she said, disappearing into the bathroom. She still had her hat on. I heard the lock click on the door.

Questioning my mother was like trying to hang onto space. I put away the corn flakes, milk, bananas, Wonder Bread, peanut butter and cans of Campbell's tomato soup scattered over the counter. I didn't know what else to do.

The next time I asked, she went to bed though it was only seven o'clock. I heard her moan. The sound made my hair stand up; it made my skin itch and my teeth hurt. I had to put my hands over my ears. I was afraid she would kill herself.

I watched her. I read her. I behaved. I took care of her. I wanted to be rid of her and I never wanted her out of my sight. And I swallowed my questions where they lay subdued and waiting for I did not know what.

Finally, I did what I always did when I wanted to know something. I went to my brother. I was twelve by then and looked up to Kenny at his advanced age of sixteen. Tall and street-smart, he could drive a car and work after school and figure skate at the Elysium and yell at our mother. He had already answered my questions about sex, but the answer I sought now seemed more dangerous.

"Why won't Mom ever talk about our father?" I asked him. He was in the kitchen opening a can of chicken noodle soup.

He shrugged, dumping it into a pot.

"All she ever told me was he died of pneumonia," I said.

He stopped and looked at me. "Pneumonia? That's a good one."

"What do you mean?"

"He died of murder. He was murdered."

It didn't exactly surprise me. Certain sounds and images that you collect during your life never leave you. A lowered voice in the next room. A face in a fading photograph mounted in an aunt's photo album. An averted gaze. A blurted question. Mrs. Halloway. A dream. A small brother's game. They all added up to this.

Kenny said he remembered the night, the screams, the police, the reporters, the commotion. "You can read about it in the newspapers," he said. "Downtown in the library. It's all there in the papers, everything that happened."

His telling me the truth like that made me know I loved him. When he took me with him the time he ran away from Aunt Mabel's I would have gone with him to the moon. We were Hansel and Gretel, in this thing together.

"How do you look it up?" I asked him.

He reached in the cupboard for the saltines. "By the date. They were killed on your second birthday."

"*They*? What do you mean, *they*?"

"Uncle Addie was killed with him."

I didn't know what to think about two murders on my second birthday. And who was this Uncle Addie? I had never heard of him. Was he a Jew bootlegger too? Why were they murdered? I looked at Kenny eating his soup and reading the newspaper. But I didn't ask him. I didn't want to. I didn't want to know. I should have listened to my mother. I should have let well enough alone. I left the kitchen, sorry I asked.

Seven

THE NEXT DAY was Saturday and my mother was pushing the vacuum cleaner in one of her rare frenzies of house cleaning. In the orphanage she had had to clean toilets, wash windows, repair uniforms, darn stockings, sort the laundry off the tall heated racks, collect garbage. "Housework is woman's natural occupation," the supervisor, Dr. Wolfenstein, told the girls, "and more important for females to know than history and literature."

Not in our house. When she wasn't at work or out on a date, my mother read. While dishes piled up in the sink and dust accumulated on the furniture, she read. Our cupboards held a jumble of plates, boxes of cereal (some empty), pots, books, cans of soup, magazines, old Dutch cleanser, clothespins, toilet paper. When we had any. We used newspapers. We slept in unmade beds. I went to sleep and got up randomly, ate this and that here and there, attended school when or if I pleased. Homework was ignored by both of us; I had to beg my mother to sign my report cards, and September's list of required school supplies created a monumental crisis. I didn't have gym clothes on time, or a combination lock for my locker or the assigned fabric for sewing class. No wonder I didn't like going to school. Seeing my class-mates with all their stuff made me feel bad. It gave me a stomach ache. I didn't like being reminded of the difference in our mothers, our fathers, our lives.

Since Kenny and I both grew up to be obsessive housekeepers, you'd think one of us would have come home and cleaned up the place. We were certainly old enough. But Kenny was a boy and therefore automati-cally exempt from domestic duties. (Once he wrote "dusted 1836 AD" with his finger in the dust on the end table.) And I somehow felt that if I made the beds or washed the breakfast dishes it would call attention to her faults as a mother, and I learned early on that her fragility, her rages, her asthma, made her too dangerous to criticize—it was safer to simply stare at the dishes piled up in the sink.

I wanted her to scold me for playing hooky, for my lousy grades, for not making the beds. I wanted some motherly disapproval. But it was as if I were transparent, there and not there, relegated to the edge of her real life and her secrets. She looked through me as if I didn't exist and I drifted around in a dream, going to the movies, reading in the library. And eating. I was hungry all the time, as if I had to fill a big inner space, or if I knew somehow of my mother's constant hunger in the orphanage and in an odd reversal was eating for two. I ate huge globs of peanut butter from the jar, sardines from the can mashed on Wonder Bread, handfuls of Corn Flakes from the box, an overripe apple, donuts on my way home from playing hooky, banana splits at the drugstore on the corner when I had the money, handfuls of Ritz crackers, chocolate chunks from Woolworths, Campbell's soup, cold, right out of the can. Eating made me happy. It focused me. I ate and ate and didn't put on a pound. People noticed and commented with wonder and envy. In the school cafeteria a loaded-up tray was called a Rosen lunch.

But maybe all those rules my mother grew up with in the Home choked her and she rebelled so she could breathe. Or maybe the bullets shot deep into those two young husbands that night made everything else beside the point. Still, every once in a while my mother put on an apron, tied up her hair, rolled up her sleeves and went to work. Today the apartment smelled of furniture polish and Fels Naptha soap; the furniture gleamed, the linoleum on the kitchen floor shone. Bananas and apples stood proudly in a pretty dish on the kitchen table. There was milk and ham and potato salad from the deli in the ice box, fresh bread in the bread box, cereal and canned vegetables in the cupboard, real toilet paper in the bathroom.

I filled a bowl with corn flakes and milk and sat down with the funnies in the kitchen. I got up and sliced a banana into my cereal and sat down again. I stared out the window at the milky clouds and the dusting of new, wet snow. My mind kept drifting over to Uncle Addie. Why hadn't I ever heard of him? Who was he? Did my mother have a secret brother? Was he really a Jew bootlegger, too, like Mrs. Halloway said? Two murders!

"Where's Kenny?" I shouted over the noise of the vacuum cleaner. I decided to ask him.

She turned it off and looked at me. "How would I know? He left." Her sigh was like a moan. "I told him he couldn't take the car, but look," she said, going over to the window, pointing at the curb, "it's gone. He took it. Every time I take his key away he comes up with another one." Her voice quivered. When she turned back to me her eyes were wet. I was afraid she'd start crying.

I wanted to tell her that she'd never be able to confiscate all the duplicate car keys Kenny had made and hidden around. But I didn't because she was practically hysterical when it came to Kenny. From the time he took her car joy-riding hardly able to see over the steering wheel, to now, when he stayed out late, or yelled at her, or took the car without permission, she would wail, "What's going to become of him?" weeping and wringing her hands. Looking back, I understood. In her terror he wasn't being a normal adolescent; he was his own father in the making, on his way to an early grave.

I hated when she got teary about Kenny. It made me pick up on her fear. I turned back to my corn flakes and funnies. But I still couldn't concentrate.

You can read about the murders in the library, Kenny had said.

My mother had gone back to pushing the vacuum cleaner. She had a scarf on her head that covered her hair and one of those flowered Hoover aprons. She looked ordinary now. Nice, like somebody's mother. She had wiped her eyes and calmed down; seeing her like this made me feel better, and I didn't want to spoil everything with my questions, or go downtown to look up secrets. It was a damp March day with a chilly wind blowing off the lake and I decided to stay home. I had my mother's library copy of *Crime and Punishment*. I would stay home with her and read.

I sat in the living room with the book, but I couldn't make any sense of the words in front of me. Something was pulling me away. It was my daddy. My daddy was pulling me. I felt it. As if he was whispering my name. Babbie, come on downtown. Come on. I'm waiting for you.

Yes. I would go. Some element of him was there. Something real.

Hurrying into the bedroom I opened my purse. There was enough for carfare. I tore off my jeans and t-shirt and put on my good blue dress. I wanted to look nice. Then I put my coat on so my mother wouldn't see what I was wearing. I felt like a sneak, cheating on our unspoken deal; she had made up a benign husband and father, given him an ordinary death of pneumonia and then pretended he never existed. My part of the deal, if I loved her, was to believe.

The radio's "Madame Butterfly" was turned up full volume over the racket of the vacuum cleaner and she waved to me as I left the apartment. I was sorry I had put on my coat. I wanted her to ask me where I was going in my good dress. I wanted to tell her so she would stop me.

It was a cold, damp Saturday threatening more snow, and shivering, I walked to the streetcar. The Center-Mayfield theater was just ahead. A double feature—*Top Hat* with Fred Astaire and Ginger Rogers, and a Tom Mix serial. It would be warm inside and I could spend my carfare money on a ticket and have enough left over for Cracker Jacks. I didn't want to go sneaking downtown to look up secrets in the library. I wanted the prize in the Cracker Jacks box. I wanted to be 12 years old.

But before I got to the box office I changed my mind again and went on to the streetcar stop.

Eight

CONSTRUCTED OF ELABORATELY carved stone and as imposing as a king's palace, the Cleveland Public Library is so huge you have to climb a steep flight of wide stone stairs just to reach the bank of heavy carved doors. Breathless with its grandeur I push them open; inside, the air feels as cool as marble and the light seems shined up, like silver.

I approach the woman sitting at the circular desk. She is writing something. I wait. Finally she looks up. She has gray hair and a thin mouth. Her glasses are down on her nose. "Yes?"

I clear my throat. "Old newspapers?" Asking this tight-lipped stranger for my mother's secrets makes my heart pound.

"Basement. Take the elevator or the stairs through that door," she says, pointing.

I ring for the elevator. Strange stairwells scare me.

Waiting, I see a scattering of men and women in the rooms off the marble hallway and people standing in line with their books at the check-out counter. The elevator arrives silently and I step inside. I am alone in there. I push "B." It is a short ride down that stops with a bump. The doors open. The light is different down here; browner, softer, like old sepia photographs. I see a man down the hall sitting behind a counter. It is so quiet I hear my own breathing. I feel hot. I'm actually sweating. I take off my coat and walk toward him. The man is wearing wire-rimmed glasses and a maroon sweater under his jacket. He looks up at me. His skin is as pale as if he sleeps down here. There is a drop of moisture hanging on the end of his nose.

"Yes?" he says, wiping his nose with a crumpled up handkerchief.

I am mute, afraid of his next question: Does your mother know you're here? I look around. Behind me, two men and a woman are scattered among the four or five long wooden tables, their heads bent over newspapers. The woman is writing something on a yellow pad. One of the men has red hair. The other man looks old. My mother isn't here. I breathe. I turn back to the man. Of course she isn't here.

I clear my throat. "Where are the newspapers?" I ask in a small voice.

"Fill this out." He hands me a sheet of paper from a pile on the counter.

REQUEST FORM is printed across the top in big letters. There is a list of questions asking for your name, address, telephone number, the newspapers requested, and the dates. And at the bottom, "Reason For Request." What can I say? It's a secret? I'm looking for my father? I stand there.

The man takes off his glasses. "Sit down over there and fill it out," he orders, nodding at the tables.

I walk over to a table against the wall. My footsteps sound too loud. The air smells of dust and paper and something else—damp shrouds. There are small windows overhead like gun slits yielding a slanted winter light. I hear the scraping of my chair as I sit down. I take out my pencil, and write down my name, address and telephone number. Kenny had said there were over a week of newspaper stories and I fill in the dates. I am calmer now; this isn't so bad. For "Newspapers Requested" I print, "The Cleveland Press," "The Cleveland News," "The Cleveland Plain Dealer." Chewing on my pencil I stare at "Reason For Request". Then I write, with a pounding heart, "School Project."

My hands are sweating. I get up and hand the form to the man. He puts on his glasses and looks at it while I stand there with a tight heart. I am sure he is staring at my pathetic lie. I wait for him to say school project? What school project? Get out of here with your lies!

He gets up and without a word disappears behind two swinging doors. I stand there. The quiet rings in my ears. He is calling my mother. He is calling the police. I'll be arrested and sent to reform school for lying in the library. I want to run out of there but my legs don't seem to move.

He comes back through the swinging doors with a pile of newspapers mounted on sticks and puts them on one of the tables. I follow him.

"Thank you," I manage.

I take off my coat and sit down. *The Cleveland Plain Dealer* is on top of the pile. There is a picture on the front page of a handsome young man with full lips, dark hair and deep set eyes. It is captioned, "**Louis Rosen.**"

That's my daddy! That's him! But he's so young. And alive. Even on this old yellow page. The tilt of his chin and the shine in his eyes have a kind of energy. I can feel it. I run my finger over the picture expecting heat. Staring, I see that Kenny looks just like him and to my surprise tears sting my eyes. I thought *I* looked like my daddy. I was sure of it. The four of us were squared off—my mother and brother are blue-eyed and fair-skinned, *we* are dark-eyed brunettes. But wait—there I am, too, in a picture of my mother holding a small child. I look like my baby pictures. My mother's face is softer, younger.

Turning to the front page of *The Cleveland Press*, the papers rustling in the quiet room, I see an artist's sketch of two men shooting at a couple of figures sprawled on the ground. The caption reads:

Louis Rosen and Adolph Adelson lay in Rosen's driveway, riddled with knife wounds and bullets.

I read the article:

TWO MURDERED AT EAST SIDE HOME
WIVES HEAR SIX SHOTS, FIND BODIES

The bodies of Louis Rosen and Adolph Adelson were found by their wives in the driveway of Rosen's home this morning at 12:30 AM.

Although Rosen was known as a "big time" bootlegger, informants told police that the other victim, Adolph Adelson who was married to Mrs. Rosen's sister, Della, had merely been visiting his in-laws with their baby from their home in Philadelphia and had no connection to bootlegging activities. Officials said he was either mistaken for a partner of Rosen's or murdered so he could not identify the killers.

Louis Rosen knew they were after him, informants said—for the past month he hadn't left his home.

Rosen is survived by his wife, Florence, and two children; Kenneth, age 6 and Babette, who will be two years old today. The birthday party planned by her mother and father will not be held.

Adelson was an accountant in Philadelphia where he specialized in income taxes. He served in the navy during the war and was a graduate of Wharton School of Finance of the Univer-sity of Pennsylvania. Besides his wife he is survived by his six-month-old daughter, Lucille.

I should feel something. But I don't. I read the words, I understand them. I do not miss the irony. Prohibition was repealed and anyone can buy whiskey anywhere. I read it again but these murderous events have nothing to do with me. They belong to the paper, to newsprint. The child's second birthday, the party canceled. Well, of course it was canceled. The guilty

Louis Rosen, the innocent Adolph Adelson. The young widows, Florence, and her sister, Della. The children, Kenneth, Babette, Lucille. Who are these people? It was like trying to hang onto an empty fistful of death.

There are several articles on the front page of *The Cleveland News.*

LAY SLAYING OF TWO TO RUM WAR .

HUNT RUM KING IN ROSEN MURDER .

ROSEN'S PARTNER DISAPPEARS . . .

SYNDICATES FIGHT FOR ALCOHOL TRADE.

There are sob stories, reconstruction of the crime stories, background stories of the bootlegging business. There is an artist's drawing of the killers' getaway car, a Peerless with the curtains closely drawn. There is a picture of my mother's sister, Della, and her husband, the unlucky Adolph, whose only crime was being in the wrong place at the wrong time. Or maybe marrying into our family.

Halfway down the page is a photograph of a mob milling around the funeral home with the caption:

Because of the crowds at the funeral home, Rosen's hearse had to receive the casket from a rear entrance.

And another taken at the cemetery:

In the hope of getting some clue to the killers, detectives mingled with the large crowd of mourners and curiosity seekers who attended Rosen's funeral.

The picture of the funeral stops my heart. My daddy is dead. Dead, here in the newspaper. There is his casket. He is not a secret, an idea, a whisper. He isn't dead of pneumonia or watching over me from a castle in the sky, or, as I sometimes daydreamed, hiding from the bad men somewhere, waiting for the right time to come home and rescue us. My mother found him bloody on the ground along with the poor Addie. My throat constricts and my eyes fill. Fat tears splash down on the newspaper. I find my handkerchief and blow my nose.

I realize that anyone who read the newspapers knew more about my own family than I did. I glance around. The few people still scattered at the tables are reading. Two or three are writing something. No one is looking at me.

I decide to steal the page with my daddy's picture. I want to take it home. But I hear the sound of a scraping chair as someone behind me gets up, and I'm afraid the tearing will make too much noise. I look at the man at the desk. He looks back. Doesn't he ever go to the bathroom or anything?

I am reading ten-year-old-news, the pages already brittle, but the revelation of the existence of Lucille actually in the house with Kenny and me that night is as new and fresh as a birth. I wonder if our joint loss that night means we're twinned, soul sisters, born of our slain fathers' blood. I wonder if our destiny is mirrored. If we look alike. If she knows about us. If she hates the family that robbed her of her father. She would be eleven, now, a year younger than I. Sitting there staring at her mother's picture, I vow that when I am grown up I will find her.

I look around. Except for the man at the desk, I'm alone. I have no idea how long I have been sitting here, reading. There is no clock on the wall. My throat hurts as if I've been yelling or crying. I need air. I wish I could go back to my pre-newspaper innocence before I viewed the corpses.

I don't want to take my father's picture home

anymore. I don't want to be his daughter anymore, either. I want him to be dead of pneumonia where it is easy to love him.

When I got home, the apartment reeked of aftershave and perfume.

"Babbie, is that you?" My mother called from the bedroom. "Where were you?"

I wanted to tell her. "Downtown! And Mom—"

She stuck her head out of the bedroom door. "There's some chop suey in the ice box."

"Mom! Listen!" I noticed that my heart was pounding. "I've been downtown at the library, and—"

"That's nice, dear," she called, ducking back in the bedroom. "I'm running late, Milt'll be here in five minutes."

I went into the bedroom. She was sitting at her dressing table putting on mascara, the room cluttered with the high heels I almost tripped over, her good black dress hanging on the door, her camel's-hair coat on the bed, nail polish, lipsticks, her pearls and earrings scattered over the dresser, her feathered hat on the chair. I smelled the cold cream she used to wipe off the mascara, and the eye shadow she wore on dates. She dabbed perfume behind her ears as if the room wasn't stinking enough, as if the murders didn't belong to her, too. It made me mad. I wanted to yell *Don't you dare leave me in this thing alone!* But all I did was kick her shoes out of the way. Hard.

She pulled on her stockings, fastened the garters, got up from the dressing table and started pounding on the bathroom door so loud you'd think someone was chasing her. She was in her slip, her good black one, with the lace that showed off her cleavage.

Kenny dashed out of the bathroom and she disappeared inside and slammed the door. I was relieved. I hated when she walked around in front of him like that.

Kenny winked at me and rushed out of the apartment.

The doorbell rang.

I opened the door to Milton Strauss.

"Kenny must have some hot date," he said, "damn near knocked me down." Once briefly a municipal judge and known thereafter and proudly as Judge Strauss, Milt was short with a wide face and bushy eyebrows. He wore loud suits and smoked cigars, and looked more like a gambler than a judge. He was my mother's boyfriend on and off for years, maybe ten, but in those days people pretended single women were as celibate as nuns.

Every February Milt sent us a flat box of candied fruits from Miami Beach. It had a little pick to spear them up. He always sent the same thing and it always made my mother mad. It was not what she wanted from him.

We wanted Milt to marry our mother. Kenny let him win at chess, I tried to be charming, we did our best. Sometimes I daydreamed that they'd come home from a date and announce that they had driven to Kentucky or somewhere and got married. I didn't exactly imagine them in love. My mother could shine up to a man and flirt and be excited, but I couldn't imagine her actually falling in love like people in books and movies. No, she would marry Milt to give Kenny and me a daddy and he would balance our lopsided family and anchor my mother who was out there somewhere swirling in orbit, scaring me. I imagined her in a demure blue silk dress and pretty picture hat with an orchid corsage pinned to her shoulder; me in my good print and Mary Jancs; Kenny and Milt in nice suits and boutonnieres. My mother and Milt would exchange rings and kiss and we would be saved. I'd have my own room. I'd have a dog and a bike. My mother would come to PTA meetings, we'd stay in one place and I could stop thinking about murder.

But he married someone else—it seemed to us, suddenly—and true to our mother's habit of tight silence about anything that really mattered, we never knew if she was the rejector or the rejected. When I was grown and married and belonged to the same country club as Milt he pretended not to see me in the dining room.

Milt strode into the apartment and plopped himself into the easy chair. He didn't just sit in a chair, he took deep, intimate possession of it like a man coming home. It made the change fall out of his pocket. Every time he left, Kenny and I lifted the seat cushion and split the loot.

"So Babbie, how's school?" he said. He smelled of cigar smoke.

My mother hurried into the living room carrying her coat. "There's some Danish in the bread box," she said, kissing me on my cheek. Her breath smelled of mouthwash. Milt helped her on with her coat and they hurried out the door, my mother's hard high heels clicking on the tile hallway.

Feeling disoriented, I went into the kitchen. Even the familiar ice-box and stove, the cracked enamel table, the kitchen sink, seemed like something lost. I opened the icebox and stood staring at the white carton of chop suey. But I didn't feel like eating; my stomach felt somewhere too near my throat, as if it would be dangerous to open my mouth. I didn't even feel like looking for Milt's change in the chair. It was as if I were alone in a weird no-man's-land that existed somewhere between this small apartment that smelled of chop suey and perfume, and that room in the basement of the Cleveland Public Library with my daddy and windows like gun slits. My isolation seemed so strange and yet so utterly familiar that I felt something drop inside me, as if I were going down in a fast elevator.

I closed the icebox, went into the living room and turned on the radio. My mother liked Gabriel Heater delivering the news and Fred Allen. Mrs. Nussbaum talking to Fred Allen with her Jewish accent always made her laugh. But my favorite program was *Mr. Kean, Tracer of Lost Persons*, with *Major Bowes* second. I turned on the radio. *Amos & Andy*. I liked *Amos & Andy*, too, but I turned it off. Listening to the radio felt wrong. Listening to the radio belonged to the time before I sat reading up on murder in the library.

I dropped into the easy chair feeling as tired as if I'd been up for days, weeks, years; as if I'd just lived my daddy's life, and mine, too. The newspapers had lifted a darkness like a curtain opening to a stage of ghosts, and I began to feel a hint of release and relief. My poor daddy—neither a god nor a devil. The truth I had discovered about him told me things I hadn't figured out yet; I only knew I felt less lonely and more lonely, free of my father and stuck with him forever.

Over the years when my mother was asked why, widowed at 27, she never remarried, she said it was because a stepfather might not be good to her children. Even though I hated to think it was my fault she was alone, and even though it made me feel guilty, I actually believed that fiction. I wanted to. I liked thinking I had a mom who loved me that much.

But the truth is she didn't marry again because her life had traumatized her into the ether where relationships can't breathe. She saw men either in candlelight or blazing daylight, in either awe or contempt, glamorized or demonized. She went from boyfriend to boyfriend and job to job and when she got older and there were no more boyfriends or jobs she turned to Kenny and me and clung with the awesome intensity of a woman who had survived the personal havoc of her century: her immigrant parents and Dickensian childhood; the violence of Prohibition and the nihilism of the Roaring Twenties; the despair of the Great Depression. And maybe worst of all, the complete indifference of the world.

Tough and damaged, she laid claim to us in her life-long widowhood and wouldn't let go. Kenny never came home after college. But I had to escape into marriage.

Nine

"GOOD AFTERNOON," DR. Herman says. "Come in."

After coming to this office every day for over a year, the twenty blocks that separate it from home is turning into a chasm. Traveling back and forth between Nate's universe and the world of my past; from one sparsely furnished office, to 15 elegant rooms; from feeling worthless and displaced in a luxurious bed, to a hard narrow couch that is beginning to feel like a fit; I am becoming two people living in conflicting worlds. The angry husband, the big house, have nothing to do with me; this couch is as real as bread. The past is present, pulsing, alive; the present as false as if I am walking through a dream like a misfit, out of sync. I have fallen through the looking glass, fallen out of time.

Entering the office I stop midway and stare at Dr. Jacob Herman. He looks back at me, bemused, waiting for me to settle down on the couch. He isn't that ordinary-looking, after all. Forget the idea of the man on the bus. He looks pretty good. He looks terrific.

"I had a dream about you," I say, after I lie down and he takes his seat.

"Last night?"

"No, as a matter of fact it was a couple of weeks ago."

"Why the wait?"

"I was too embarrassed."

"But you're not too embarrassed now?"

"No. Well, a little. But I'm ready to tell you. I made up my mind."

"Go on."

"Well," I begin, "in the dream I come into your office and except for a cameo on a velvet ribbon around my throat, I'm naked. I lie down on the couch. What are you thinking? you say. I say I'm thinking I'm naked. And I laugh and then I cry."

"Then what?"

"Then I woke up. Aroused. Moist. Appalled. My heart pounding."

"Tell me about the cameo you wore in the dream."

"Nate gave me that."

"A cameo's a face, isn't it? A watching face. Why do you think you'd wear Nate's watching face to seduce me?"

"I haven't the faintest idea."

"What were you feeling in the dream?"

"Sick with lust, moaning with it," I say, glad for once that we're not facing each other.

"What else?"

"What else? Rejected. I was feeling rejected."

"Because I didn't have sex with you?"

"Well, yes, I'd say something like that would make you feel rejected."

"So you're angry."

"Over a dream? Don't be silly."

"You sound angry. Maybe it's something else you want from me that you're not getting."

"Yeah, like how to fix my life. Like doing what I'm paying you for." I rub my head. I didn't mean to say that. "Look, Jacob, it's not your fault. I told you I was too stupid to do this."

"So if you haven't the brains to get anywhere with me, you might as well try your body?"

"That didn't get me anywhere either, did it?"

I think of sex with Nate. Of how I like it. Love it. Sex is how I know I am alive, married, a mother. I desire Nate, his weight, his smell, his body, his arrogance, his supreme confidence. His desire. I desire his desire. Later, out of bed, I am faced again with his stony silence and contempt, but in bed, in the dark with the shades drawn against the black night and my shame, I don't

93

care. Nate's passion transports me out of myself; I am different, worthwhile. Wanted.

(The sex was the last to go. When I began sleeping on a narrow couch in my dressing room, we both knew the marriage was over. I couldn't bear his touch, his proximity, his breath on my skin.)

"What are you thinking about?" Dr. Herman asks.

"Sex."

"But your dream isn't about sex. It's about the opposite. You can flirt and seduce and go naked, but you've made sure Nate's around your neck to stop you from getting involved with anyone else."

"But he makes me miserable!"

"Maybe that's the point."

"The point?"

"The point is you married a man who makes you miserable, a man who can therefore keep you safe from love and the pain of loss, the way you loved and lost your father."

His words make me remember another desire; a longing deeper than sex and as indescribable as happiness or true love. I didn't know then how treacherous, how misleading, such ordinary and eager dreams would be for me, or the way yearning and lust and murder were all bound up in my young soul.

He clears his throat. "Our time's up."

Ten

WHEN I TURNED seventeen my mother did a sort of double take as if she had never seen me before. She hustled me into the modeling life. "I was smart in school," she said, "and look where it got me. It's better to be like you." Meaning, of course, dumb. "Use your looks," she told me, leaving it unsaid, but clear: that's all you have.

So she pulled me out of school in the twelfth grade and we made the rounds of photographers and department stores and shops.

We had first gone to the principal's office for the necessary severance. Mr. Morley took us into his office. He looked busy and distracted. It was September; school was starting in four days. A typewriter clattered in the office next door.

"I'm Florence Rosen," she said, holding out her hand. "And of course you know my daughter."

He glanced at me. "Twelve B?"

"Twelve A."

"So you graduate this January."

"Mr. Morley," my mother said, "that's what we came to see you about."

"Please sit down." He gestured at the two hard chairs facing his desk, and settled into his seat. The room smelled of paper and stale coffee.

"My daughter has been hired to model at Milgrims," she said, smiling.

I stared at her. I hated when she lied. Especially to the principal of Heights High. I had no modeling job and didn't expect to get one. But she kept on smiling sweetly at Mr. Morley as if I wasn't sitting there glaring at her. "I hate to take her out of school," she said, turning on the charm, "but really, these days there aren't

many jobs out there for a 17-year-old, are there?"
Sighing, she leaned back in her chair. "And since she
isn't much of a student, don't you think she's better off
working?"

I squirmed in my chair. I wasn't exactly opposed to
leaving school, but I wasn't crazy about sitting here
while my mother reminded the principal of my rotten
grades. I had been skipping school since third grade. Or
I'd get there so late the crossing guard would be gone.
Why not? School seemed after the fact; irrelevant,
trivial. Besides, as a co-keeper of family secrets it was
important to be stupid. My mother expected it, my aunts
and cousins, my teachers. And so did I. I believed in my
dumbness. It was too dangerous to think.

I was in awe of Mr. Morley with his white mustache
and stern manner. All the kids were. No way would he
let me quit school. You only have one semester to go!
he'll say. If you leave you'll regret it for the rest of your
life! I relaxed, breathing. Mr. Morley will save me from
my mother.

But this aloof, frightening sage was nodding and
smiling back at her. "Well yes, these are difficult times.
Tough times. And a job's a job. Yes indeed." He turned
to me. "Will you be walking down a flight of stairs in a
gorgeous gown?"

I was too astonished to speak. Or move. But my
mother was getting up and shaking hands with Mr.
Morley, who had stood and walked around his desk.

And I was a school dropout. They stood waiting for
me to get up, but convinced of my dumbness and worthlessness by this consensus of two who should know, I
sat there, stunned and ashamed. Mr. Morley and my
mother were beaming at me now, as if they had just
given me something.

Going home in the car my mother was full of plans
and strategies for my transition from schoolgirl to
model. I sat, listening. It had never occurred to me to

defy her about anything and it still didn't. It was easier to know what she wanted and needed me to be, than to know what I wanted and needed to be.

The only person upset that I quit school was my Uncle Sid. I loved him for that. He even came over and talked to my mother, but she told him to mind his own goddamn business.

Married to Sally, my father's sister, he wasn't even my real uncle, but he was the only adult male in my life and when I married I appointed him to walk me down the aisle, bypassing my real uncle, Marvin. He told my husband, "You better be good to her—I gave her away and I can take her back." I loved him for that, too.

Uncle Sid was like a Jewish Monty Wooley, the movie actor from the forties who usually played an irascible grouch who hated children and dogs. His character would articulately insult everyone, but underneath you knew he was a softy. Uncle Sid was like that.

"What kind of slop is this!" He would shout to his poor wife when she tried to serve him something normal, like lamb chops or chicken. He only liked chili con carne and herring in sour cream with boiled potatoes, so Aunt Sally would sigh and go back to fixing two meals; a regular one for the children and another for Sid. Because of him I've had a lifelong love of chili.

His voice was rough as sandpaper, as if he had polyps in his throat—which he actually did, and eventually had removed. After the operation he wasn't allowed to talk for awhile, which gave his wife and daughters a welcome reprieve from his bellowing. He was tall, maybe six feet, with a headful of gray hair, a curved nose, and a half-chewed cigar stuck in his mouth. When he wasn't on the phone with his bookie playing the horses he had loud opinions on everything and was usually right. He was the first person I ever heard say we should get out of Viet Nam. He said it right from the beginning, even before the protesters.

He talked to me about my father, too, then the only relative who would. He told me that when he needed money to set up his CPA practice everyone in the family turned him down except my father, who gave him the money without a question. He told me the same story over and over as if it was the only good thing he could think of to say about him. But I never got tired of hearing it.

One December he invited me to go with him and his family to Miami Beach for Christmas vacation, where they had rented an apartment. I was beside myself with joy; to be invited to the sunny, glamorous, fantasy land of Miami Beach was a gift beyond my wildest dreams. Aunt Sally had left earlier on the train, and driving down, my cousins Betty and Jean and I took turns sitting in the front seat. The highway hummed with cars and trucks as the daily landscape changed from gray slush to brown, and on the third day, to a thrilling green. By then Betty and Jean were restless, whining with boredom, but I felt at home in motion. I was used to movement. I'd been in motion all of my life. When it was my turn to sit by the window I wound it down and inhaled the gentle air as if its sunny warmth could give me something I craved of the world.

During the four-day trip it became painfully apparent that my cousins didn't want me there. I couldn't understand their resentment of their father's affection toward me—after all, he was *their* father. And when we arrived in Miami, stiff and mussed, it was equally obvious that my Aunt Sally didn't want me there, either. Since the dinner table was set with only four places I realized that my presence was a complete surprise to her. I also understood in that instant that if Uncle Sid had told her that he wanted to bring me, she would have vetoed the idea. As soon as she saw me she set another place, but I saw her give Uncle Sid a look. Afraid I'd start crying in front of them, I went into the bathroom and locked the door. Sitting on the hard edge of the bathtub, wishing with all my heart that I hadn't come, I choked tears until Betty banged on the door and told me to come out, dinner was ready. I put some cold water on my face, breathed, and unlocked the door.

The table had a pretty blue cloth and real linen napkins. Wonderful smells wafted out of the kitchen. The five of us sat down together with Aunt Sally and Uncle Sid at the head and foot of the table. While Uncle Sid had his herring and boiled potatoes, we ate fried chicken, mashed potatoes and green beans. Warm rolls. Apple pie with ice cream. It brought tears to my eyes. Once when Kenny and I were grown I asked him if he ever remembered the three of us sitting down together to a meal at home. After a long pause, during which I supposed he was thinking, he said no.

A few weeks later he called me. "Babbie, do you remember if we ever sat down to a meal together at home?"

"I already asked you that!" I cried.

Everyone was quiet during dinner. I couldn't wait to get out of there. After Betty, Jean and I did the dishes, also in silence, I asked Uncle Sid if I could go out for awhile.

"Be back by nine," he mumbled from behind his newspaper.

As I left the apartment in my light summer dress, the tropical air seemed to caress my skin. Driving down, we had shed a layer of our winter clothes each day—first our hats and mittens, then coats, then on the last day, our sweaters. Now, after the mean bite of Cleveland's winter, it was thrilling just to feel the soft air and smell the salty ocean. I stopped at an orange juice stand that had more oranges piled up than I had ever seen in my life, and drank the sweet, cool juice in a gulp. A drugstore was two doors away. I went in, bought a chocolate ice cream cone, and stood at the newsstand, licking my cone and reading comics. Coming out I heard the faint strains of music, and following it, found myself in front of the Rooney Plaza Hotel.

Surrounded by palm trees, graceful archways and purple and pink bougainvillea, the hotel seemed so glamorous I walked around to the side to get a closer look. Standing on one of the brick paths leading from the golf course I watched the elegant ladies and gentlemen dine on the patio as waiters in tuxedos glided gracefully around the candlelit tables. A woman in an upswept hairdo and sparkling earrings leaned forward as her escort lit her cigarette. A couple clinked their wine glasses. A pretty blonde lady was laughing among a table of six. Music from inside drifted into the fragrant air—a man was actually singing "Moon Over Miami."

There was a huge yellow moon overhead just like in the song, and I stood listening to the clink of china and murmur of voices, smelling the tantalizing aroma of steak and garlic. Now the man was singing "Dancing Cheek to Cheek."

"Hi" I heard someone say. I turned and saw a boy about my age with freckles and red hair.

"Hi," I said.

He told me his name was Derrick McNeil, but everyone called him Mac. He lived in Miami Beach.

"Do you want to see me do something?" he said.

"Okay."

I watched as he crept up to the patio on his hands and knees, darted to one of the empty tables, stuck a white napkin and a spoon into his pocket and crept back to me.

"Now you do it," he said, grinning

I shook my head.

"Come on," he said again. "It's easy. Watch."

And he did it again. It did look easy.

"I'm afraid I'll get caught," I told him, when he came back with more stuff in his pockets—this time a pair of salt and pepper shakers.

"Nah," he said. "You won't get caught. They're pretty dumb in there."

So I did it. Ashamed and exhilarated I crawled up to the patio, stole a whisky glass and butter knife, and raced back to Mac.

"You stood up too soon," he said. "You have to stay down where they can't see you."

My heart was pounding.

"Hey, look!" he said, pointing.

A couple had got up from their seats and were walking into the dining room to dance. The lady's purse was dangling on her chair.

"I'm gonna get it," Mac said.

"No!" I said. "Not someone's purse!"

But he was already down on all fours. In a moment his hand was on the purse and in another instant the waiter eyed him and started yelling.

Mac ran like the wind, the purse dangling on his arm. "Come on!" he gasped, grabbing my hand. We ran and ran deep into the dark golf course until I tripped on something sharp and fell. Mac got on top of me. It wasn't like with Frankie. Feeling the length of his body pressed upon mine was like coming home. Suddenly aware of my body, my skin, the way the air smelled, the way I smelled, we kissed and kissed. It was exciting, thrilling. He touched my breast. I let him. My knee began to throb. I looked down. It was dripping blood. Mac took the napkin he had stolen out of his pocket and tied it around my knee. I got up, limping.

He said he'd take me to a different place the next night. "Meet me in front of the Rooney Plaza at 8. Okay?"

"Okay."

"Promise?"

I promised. The two of us were out here on our own. Aunt Sally and Betty and Jean didn't want me, but Mac did. Mac was my soul mate.

When I limped back to the apartment, they were waiting for me.

"Do you know what time it is?" Uncle Sid shouted.

I shook my head. I never knew what time it was.

"It's after 11!" he bellowed. "We've been frantic! I was about to call the police!"

"Your knee!" Aunt Sally cried.

I looked down. Blood had soaked through the napkin. "I fell."

She took me into the bathroom, sat me down, and gently washed the wound. "This is going to hurt a little," she said, dabbing iodine on it while I yelled.

"Shh," she whispered. "You'll wake the girls." I watched her wind a bandage around my knee. A year ago when I fell off the swing after school and gashed my elbow no one was home and I bled all over the bathroom. I ran cold water on it, wrapped it in a towel and stuck a bunch of band aids on it, but it got infected anyway—at school the next day my elbow was hot and throbbing and Miss Brooks sent me to the nurse. And here was Aunt Sally, who didn't even want me there, tenderly bandaging my knee as if I were Betty or Jean. I felt my eyes fill.

She looked at me. "Does it hurt, honey?"

I wiped my eyes on a piece of toilet paper, but all I could do was shake my head.

While she was cutting adhesive tape Uncle Sid came in. I couldn't look at him. I felt too bad to even look at him. I was afraid he wouldn't like me any more.

"You will not leave this apartment. Do you understand?"

I couldn't speak.

"Do you?" he yelled.

"Sid, shh, the girls," Aunt Sally said.

"Do you understand!" he hissed.

"Yes," I whispered.

"Yes what?"

"Yes I understand."

"You're grounded. Now go to bed."

Grounded! Other kids were grounded, not me. No one had ever grounded me. I thought of Mac and felt my heart bang in shame and then swell with relief—I couldn't keep our date tomorrow! I wasn't allowed! I was grounded! Surprised, I went to my bed on the living room couch.

But I couldn't sleep. I was feeling something too new and strange to sleep. As if I had finally been allowed inside the stronghold. As if Uncle Sid had taken my hand and pulled me back from the abyss. I thought of Mac lying on top of me on the golf course. I touched my breast, remembering the thrill of his hand there. I had wanted more. But not now. Not any more. Not after Uncle Sid. He cared about me, he worried about me, he was going to call the police to find me! I realized I didn't want to run wild and steal and be Mac's soul mate. And now I didn't have to. I was *grounded*. My knee was hurting, but feeling like someone's daughter, I turned over and fell into a deep sleep.

Eleven

MY MOTHER HAD made a list of likely department stores and shops and photographers and we made the rounds. To my surprise, I was hired by Halle's to model in its tearoom at lunchtime, by Higbee's and May's for their fashion shows, photographer Harry Cole for his fashion shoots and catalogues, and by Quinn-Maas, an exclusive specialty shop. I strutted on runways, stretched my legs and pointed my toes in the new nylon hose for the photographer, and (in fashion's convoluted calendar) posed in fur coats and rivers of sweat in July, and bathing suits and goose bumps in January. I demonstrated vacuum cleaners at conventions, sprayed cologne at ladies in department stores, paced runways in my new hip-swinging stride, all the while feeling an immense sorrow. I had become my mother's creation, her idea of me, a no-brainer not even fit to finish high school, a moving, speaking, walking size 8, her windup girl-toy, an early, pioneering Barbie, pushed down the road of her vicarious fantasies. With no idea of who I was or wanted to be, I went along, riveted by her will as she sat in the dark corner of the photographer's studio, the front row of the style shows, the table in the tearoom.

Backstage I changed my outfits in 40 seconds. Or rather the two dressers did, one of them stripping the clothes off my back while the other pulled the next change over my head. They grabbed the shoes from my feet, thrusting my toes into another pair (you hold onto the dresser's back for balance), hung my neck with jewelry, patted down my hair and there I was, out on the runway again. 40 seconds flat. If it was a swimsuit show you were stripped naked but no one looked at you, not even the male buyers and merchandisers who happened to be milling around backstage. They'd watch the audience through a part in the curtain, or appraise the clothes hanging on racks, or ask someone why numbers 26, 14 and 43 weren't in the show. Sometimes I'd catch a stock boy sneaking a look, but I didn't care. I wasn't a real live woman.

Every day from twelve to two I modeled in Halle's tea room. In the dressing room, staring at my reflection, the stranger in the mirror looking back at me with the breasts and shimmering silver gown and silver sandals seemed to have emerged overnight, willed into being by my mother. Modeling among the tables in Adrian suits with John Frederick hats, Norell gowns with silver fox jackets, Rubinstein dresses under mink, the lunching ladies and I eyed each other with envy—they for my so-called glamorous job, me for their different destinies. And the chic clothes on their backs that didn't belong to the Halle Bros. Company. And the delicious-looking chicken pot pies and seafood crepes and chocolate mousses on their plates that made my stomach growl. I envied them because they were sitting down and their feet didn't hurt. But mostly I envied them for their mothers, nicely lunching with them or at home minding their own business. Their mothers weren't like mine. I could tell. I hated them for it.

My mother was watching me from her usual corner table. She came on her lunch hour every day and ordered the welsh rarebit, or a tuna sandwich. Sometimes she had a fresh fruit plate and if it was a cool day, the beef stew. She always had butter pecan ice cream for dessert and she always complained that they served it in a warm dish, making it melt.

After her lunch my mother paid her check using my employees' discount. Then she went into the Ladies, and emerged with fresh lipstick, her hair combed and her hat just so. She looked good.

She often told me how vain her mother was—when I was four or five I remember watching Grandma Anna sit in front of the mirror and do up her long auburn hair with hairpins that I thought, in fascinated horror, went inside her skull. But my mother was vain, too, especially about her hair. Even during the Depression she went to a beauty shop once a week for a shampoo and a set with sticky lotion. It cost fifty cents, and although fifty cents could also buy a meal in those days, after having had her hair cut off in the Home, my mother would rather get her hair done. Alberta's Beauty Salon had stacks of dog-eared magazines called *Silver Screen* and *Movie Lives* and a tall permanent-wave machine that looked like a Martian engine of torture with its metal helmet growing wires out of a wheeled stand.

Once on the rare occasion that my mother spoke about her years in the orphanage, she said that when her class graduated the girls were given pretty white dresses for the ceremony and that after living in a scratchy second-hand uniform for twelve years the dress was like a gift from a fairy godmother. But after the ceremony they took the dresses back, breaking her heart.

When I got to be twelve or thirteen she would sometimes fasten her eyes on me, announce that I needed a new dress and away we would go to May's Girls' Department. Summarily dismissing the approaching saleslady with an imperious wave of her hand, she'd leaf through the sale racks like a store executive and bring an armload to the fitting room where I stood waiting obediently in my slip. I tried on the dresses she selected as she zipped and buttoned, straightened shoulders, tied bows and patted down my hair as if I were a plastic doll. I let her. Shopping always got her in a good mood. It was her show, she was in charge. I didn't mind. I had her attention. Shopping was one of the things mothers did with their daughters, but in my case, it was pretty nearly the only thing, and I liked it. I loved it.

Some of her love of clothes seemed to spill over to me. Although I can't tell you what my new dress looked like, I can recall perfectly the smile on my mother's face and the way her eyes shone and the feel of her hands on my hair and the sound her bracelets made as she moved the hangers on the rack. I can still smell the stale perfume in the fitting room and see the dismissed, disapproving saleslady standing in her black oxfords with her arms folded and her glasses glittering in the light that slanted through the big dirty windows. In the car on the way home, my mother had me open the box and shake the dress out of its tissue paper so she could look at it again.

But I was vain, too. If you were female and father-less and powerless and uneducated and broke, you understood it was your only shot. (My mother never said poor; we were broke.) And when I began modeling and noticed people, boys, grown men, looking at me, I figured it was the start of something, some kind of power. So I painted my toenails, got permanents, shaved my legs, practiced makeup, and sweated in the sun for a tan, turning myself as methodically as steak on a grill. I shopped for bargains and sucked in my stomach and practiced good posture and liked whomever asked me out, even if I didn't.

Now I was the one who was dating and my mother was the one being left home alone. Narrow-eyed, she watched me get ready for a date, criticizing my dress, my hair, my earrings. She'd choose another outfit, instruct me to take a coat, no not that one, it's the wrong length for your dress. She told me to change my shoes, straighten my stocking seams, take an umbrella. She tilted my hat to a different angle and said to watch when I sat down that my slip didn't show. She drove me crazy.

Finally I ran out of the apartment and waited downstairs on the sidewalk.

Coming home, sometimes I found her waiting for me outside the apartment with a coat thrown over her nightgown.

"Isn't that your mother?" Nate asked one night as we pulled up.

"No," I lied, watching her pace back and forth. "Go on Nate, I'll see myself in."

My legs heavy with dread, I dragged myself out of the car and approached her.

"Where have you been!" she roared, as Nate drove off.

I backed away. I knew what was coming. "Miriam's party—then we went to Clark's for hamburgers . . . ."

"Do you know what time it is!" she screamed, rearing up and stretching her finger at me like royalty gone mad. "I've got to go to work in the morning!"

"You should have gone to bed . . . ."

"Gone to bed!" She shrieked. "Gone to bed! With you out there! Doing God knows what! Look at you! Look at your hair!"

"Mom, shhh, let's go inside—"

"Don't you tell me what to do! I've been waiting for hours! Hours! Insane with worry!" she screamed, waving her arms so that her coat flew open and her nightgown strap slipped down, exposing her breast.

I pulled her coat around her. There was snow on the ground but she smelled of sweat. I grabbed her elbow to steer her inside, but she shook me loose, rolling her eyes like a dangerous animal. "Don't touch me!"

"Mom, please, the neighbors . . . ."

She stretched her mouth wide. "The neighbors!" She hollered. "The neighbors! All you care about are the neighbors! What about *me*!" Hands like claws, she lunged at me and pulled her nails down my cheek.

My face stung. I touched it. There was blood on my finger.

"Hey, shut up down there!" someone called from a window.

It was Mr. Cousins from 4-B. I recognized his voice.

I wanted to shake her. I wanted to grab her by her hair and yank her inside. But I headed into the building, hoping she'd follow me. Sometimes that worked. Unlocking the door I stood there, holding it open like a Park Avenue doorman. I stood, waiting. Mr. Cousins window slammed shut. A truck rumbled by. She regarded me suspiciously from the sidewalk like a vigilant guard dog. Then, keeping her distance, she walked past me in slow motion showing her teeth. I waited motionlessly at the door eying her as carefully as a matador watching the bull.

"Let's go in and make a cup of tea," I said.

She laughed insanely.

"Babbie!" Mrs. Rubin, yelled from upstairs, "You want I should call the police?"

"No, no, Mrs. Rubin it's okay," I called, feeling my stinging face heat up.

A voice boomed down I didn't recognize. "For God's sake if you don't shut up down there *I'm* calling the police!"

I left the door and moving cautiously approached my mother. I took her arm. She jerked it away. I grabbed her wrist and holding on as if she were a misbehaving two-year-old, pulled her inside.

In the light I saw that her eyes were bloodshot and her skin had red blotches. Her hair stood on end as if she had racked her fingers through it again and again. She looked like a lunatic. I managed to get her up the stairs to our apartment; inside, she collapsed on the couch and started to moan.

I never knew what to do when she got like this. She was my mother but she wasn't, as if she had been invaded by some raving stranger who just looked like her. When I was a child I'd hide in the closet in terror while she raged, but now she made me furious. Now I wanted to shake her until her teeth rattled—and in the next instant to put my arms around her and rub her back. But what scared me now was the realization that she was as helpless as I.

I tried to put a cool washcloth on her face. She pushed me away, but at least she stopped wailing. I made a cup of tea and poured some whiskey into it. She knocked it out of my hand spilling tea all over the coffee table. I mopped it up with a dishtowel. My face was stinging. I was exhausted. I left her and went to bed.

The next morning when I came into the kitchen the coffee pot was perking away on the stove filling the kitchen with its aroma. Neatly dressed in her navy blue suit and matching felt hat that dipped over one eye, smelling nicely of her lilac bath powder, my mother was setting the table, pouring orange juice, making toast.

"Good morning," she said, without a trace of embarrassment or apology, as if just hours before she hadn't been acting like a lunatic, as if my face didn't have long red welts from her clawing fingernails, as if the neighbors weren't about to call the police, or that she hadn't been outside in her nightgown with her breast exposed screaming like a maenad. I stared at her. Was it me? Was I losing it?

"I've got to run, Babbie," she said, putting on her coat. "Meet me at Mills for dinner tonight? Six-thirty okay? Or would you rather go to Wong's?"

I just looked at her.

"I'll call you later," she said, walking briskly out of the apartment, looking every inch the efficient, attractive, businesswoman on the go.

After she left I sat at the kitchen table drinking coffee and wondering if makeup would cover the scratches on my face so I could go to work.

She needn't have worried about my virtue, if that's what it was. Mired in the repressed secrets of my perennially single mother, I was still virginal, unaffected by the lustful gropings of this young man or that in the back seats of cars. Their lips smashed against mine, their tongues thrust in my mouth, their hot breath in my ear, I felt their rough cheeks rubbing my face red, their hands on my breasts. Eighteen years old, I pushed them away with a child's stunted appetite. I registered my own inhibition—a word the rejected boys flung at me in their frustration and anger—with something like awe; for all their heavy breathing and eager lust, these boys were lifeless to me, irrelevant, reduced to plastic or cardboard, as sexless as I found myself in front of the cameras and on runways.

What I wanted to do was talk about my father. Sometimes, in pride and shame, I would blurt out the whole murderous tale, gratuitously and out of context, even to new acquaintances. But although I told Bobby and Arlene, and then Roger, and later Virginia, one of my co-models at Halle's, the only response I ever got from anyone was a nod or a change of subject; it was as if the world was conspiring with my mother in silence.

I didn't know what I expected from my lurid confessions, but if the murders were no big deal, where did that put the secret that had haunted my family for sixteen years? Did the shame I seemed eager to flaunt embarrass them? Was that it? Or was it as if they passed a wreck on the road and looked away from the carnage? Or maybe they already knew. Maybe I was giving them old news—hadn't the murders been all over the newspapers?

I wanted to find out from others what I couldn't at home. I wanted to know if Lou was bad and it served him right, or if he merely got caught making a youthful mistake. I wanted to know if it was okay to love him. I wanted to know if I hated him. I wanted to know if I had to worry about having, or passing on, an inherited criminal trait.

So I went back downtown to the library. I was now eighteen years old; it had been six years since I sat there reading about the murders. I thought I had digested the information I sought and gone on with my life. But my memory of the story clung to me with an energy and afterlife that regurgitated like indigestion. It made me uneasy. It interfered with my days. I was no longer twelve years old. I needed to know more.

Twelve

THE WOMAN AT the library information desk directed me to the basement again but when I got there the room looked different—sort of shrunken, the way your elementary school seems when you go back as an adult. There were more tables than I remembered and the light looked different—clearer and brighter. It smelled different, too, fresher, maybe, or newer. The windows like gun slits were gone—or had I imagined them? A middle-aged woman with blonde hair sat at the counter where the man with the runny nose had been.

She handed me a questionnaire from the pile on the counter and I sat down and began filling it out. I wrote the names of the newspapers I wanted, and the dates. Then I saw: "Reason For Request," and felt the same panic of six years ago. Stop this, I told myself. You are not twelve years old. Boldly, I wrote "Family Murders." Feeling my face heat up, I erased it and wrote, "Father's Death." I looked up at the woman behind the counter. She was writing on an index card as if she smelled something bad. She reminded me of my seventh grade gym teacher who thought she was a drill sergeant; I couldn't imagine handing it to her. I erased "Father's Death" and wrote "Research." There was a place to check if you wanted photocopies of the requested material. Photocopies! I could get copies!

I gave the woman at the desk the form and waited as she read it.

"The copies will be $15," she said.

$15 for my daddy. Cutting-edge technology. I could be his keeper.

I handed over the money.

"Come back at four o'clock," she said.

It was before the era of microfilm and when I returned I found a pile of large, heavy sheets stacked up on the counter with my name on top. The print was blown up on thick, cumbersome pages and magnified so many times it was as if the words would jump off the page and start bleeding or screaming. My hands were sweaty and when I picked up the unwieldy papers they slipped out of my hands, spilling their secrets. The lady drill sergeant behind the counter handed me some rubber bands and I finally got them rolled up and restrained, smelling innocently of ink. They were what I had of him.

I made it home only minutes before my mother. She worked in an insurance office now, but I knew it was only a matter of time before she got mad at something or someone and quit, because that's what she always did. She was so fast and smart her employers hated to see her leave, which is why she was quickly hired somewhere else.

But during the Great Depression if you were lucky enough to have a job you didn't dare quit—not even my mother. In those days she worked for the City of Cleveland in the Engineering Department, through the good offices of a councilman, whom, I learned later, had in better times been her married lover. But Cleveland was so broke it paid its employees in scrip, which looked like play money and was just about as worthless. Too embarrassed to barter her scrip at the grocery store herself, the year that I was ten she put me in the car and cruised the neighborhoods, sending me into one grocery store after another with instructions to ask if they took scrip. Over and over the answer was a shaking head or a muttered no, but sooner or later a grocer would say yes. Feeling important and triumphant I'd run proudly with the good news to my mother, waiting in her car at the curb, and she'd go inside with her scrip. Potatoes were three cents a pound, eggs a dime a dozen. If you bought day-old, bread was a nickel and you could get a whole chicken for fifty cents. Fish was even cheaper, only a quarter, but I put my foot down. I wouldn't eat the slimy thing with the staring eyes, and my mother humored me.

Clutching the rolled up photocopies, I dashed around the apartment looking for a hiding place. But they were too long for my dresser drawers, too conspicuous in the kitchen cupboard, and there wasn't enough room behind the books on the shelves. Running out of time I slid them on the top shelf of the closet my mother and I shared.

If she discovered them God knows what she would do—start crying or get an asthma attack or become furious. Her anger turned her eyes into blue flame, igniting and inspiring her mind; the unfortunate recipient of her fury could be an erring store clerk, a blundering acquaintance, a friend who disappointed her, her mother or sister or child. She had a kind of free-floating anger that could send her flying into a fight with the precise, withering vocabulary of the valedictorian and insatiable reader she was; her verbal range went beyond mere profanity into amazingly inventive insults—which I had tried hard to avoid all my young life, and which I had no intention of stirring up now.

But triggering one of her asthma attacks worried me even more than her anger. I was afraid she would die. So was she. So probably was the doctor judging by the grim look on his face every time he was summoned. Although in those days doctors made house calls, there was little Dr. Page could do except listen to her hungry breathing and rattling chest with his stethoscope and prescribe steam, which would already be bubbling away as she gasped for breath. I would go into the bathroom, sit on the edge of the bathtub and shut my eyes.

Sometimes I went outside and sat on the stoop feeling the cold concrete on my bottom. When I was nine I daydreamed that I'd run away to Cedar Point so I wouldn't have to see her die. I'd live on the beach and go on the rolling coaster and Ferris wheel. Where I'd get the money for the rides and the cotton candy and hot dogs I planned on I had no idea, but I figured I'd think of something. The only thing that stopped me was my fear that no one would come looking for me.

One time she got such a severe attack in Atlantic City, she really did almost die. I was eleven and thrilled that she had taken me along because she was always in a good mood when we traveled. As it turned out, she survived the asthma but I damn near killed us both.

We had checked into our hotel on the boardwalk and followed the bellboy to our room. It smelled of mildew and there was a sprinkling of sand on the floor. After he left with his tip, she began unpacking, carefully hanging up the new dress she had bought for the trip, laying out her bathing suit and beach robe, arranging toilet articles in the bathroom. But I couldn't wait to get in the water and pestered her until she said I could go on ahead.

"I'll see you on the beach," she said, fishing out my bathing suit from the suitcase.

"How soon?" I asked, changing.

"As soon as I finish unpacking. Go to the beach in front of the hotel and stay there so I can find you."

I grabbed a towel and ran out the door.

"Babbie!" she called after me. "Did you hear me?"

"Yeah."

"Right in front! And don't go in the water 'til I get there!"

"Okay! Okay!" I said, hurrying to the elevator.

"Come back here," she ordered.

"What now?" I said, returning to the room.

"Don't you take that tone with me, young lady." She was shaking a bottle of sun tan oil. "Turn around."

Obediently, I turned, and felt her rub the oil on my back, then my arms and legs. I looked at her in surprise. She was in one of her mother moods. I liked it. I loved it. It felt nice. I liked the feel of her hands and the cool oil on my skin.

I headed to the elevator but she pulled me back again. "You're not to go in the elevator like that. Here," she said, handing me my shirt. "Put this on. You have to look more lady-like when you go out in public." I never knew what got her into these mothering fits but it was okay with me. I'd take every one I could get.

The sand burned my feet. The air smelled of sea salt. The beach was crowded but I found a spot halfway between the boardwalk and shore, and spread out my towel.

I decided to work on my tan and stretched out. After a while I got too hot and sat up. Where was she? I was getting tired of waiting.

I looked around for cute boys but all I saw were fleshy grown-ups in beach chairs and little kids playing in the sand. The sun was so hot I started to sweat. I looked at the sparkling blue-green ocean. The surf looked just right—the waves not as fierce and scary as up in Nahant when I visited my Aunt Lill, just high enough to be fun. I decided to take a quick dip. Just to cool off.

I ran into the surf. The water was cold, salty. I swam for awhile, then I rode a wave to shore. The ride was so much fun I did it again. And again. Riding the surf over and over, playing in the perfect turquoise waves, I forgot about looking for cute boys and waiting for my mother and everything else.

But after a while I started to worry that she was on the beach searching for me. I got out of the water and dripping, ran back to my towel. She wasn't there. I looked up and down the sand. She wasn't anywhere. I had no idea how long I had been in the water, but the sun was lower and I noticed the crowd thinning as people put on robes, shook out towels and walked slowly to the wooden steps leading up to the boardwalk.

Dripping, my skin gritty with salt and sand, I went back to the hotel. I couldn't remember what room we were in and had to ask the desk clerk. I saw a clock on the wall in the lobby—four o'clock! I had left at two thirty! Where was she? Riding up in the elevator, my throat got tight.

The door was locked. I knocked and waited. I knocked again. And again. Something was wrong. My heart shriveled in fear. I heard voices behind me in the hall and saw a few girls about my age. They were running and shouting; they were going swimming with their parents; they were kids. "Mom?" I called, in a shaking voice. Finally I heard a stirring inside the room. My mother opened the door. Her face was a funny color, sort of a blue-white and she was bent over.

"Mom!"

But she didn't answer. I could see she couldn't. She was gasping too hard. She crawled back on the bed in the same dress she had traveled in. Terrified, I stared at her.

"Doctor," she gasped.

But I couldn't move.

"Telephone," she wheezed.

I grabbed the phone.

"Front desk," the man said.

"Send a doctor! We need a doctor!"

"What seems to be the trouble?"

"Please!" I begged, trying not to cry. "It's my mother! My mother's sick!"

"What's your room number?"

"Hold on!" I hollered, dropping the phone on its wire. I ran outside, looked at the door and dashed back. "509!" I yelled into the phone.

"509!"

I put a cold washcloth on my mother's forehead, but she pushed it off and waved me away. Then I remembered about the steam. Sometimes steam helped. I ran the hot water in the bathtub and sink and tried to lift her but she was too heavy. I did get her to her feet, but her legs sort of melted, and gasping, she collapsed back on the bed. I smelled her sweat. As I was trying to wave the steam into the bedroom with a towel, I heard the doctor's knock on the door. It seemed as if I'd been waiting an hour but it was probably no more than 20 minutes or so.

Although the doctor was the most welcome sight of my young life, all I saw of him was his stethoscope on my mother's chest and back, and the somber look on his face.

He turned to me. "How old are you?"

"Eleven," I whispered.

"Okay, young lady, get your mother out of this room and out of Atlantic City. Something here is making her very sick."

I looked at her. "But I don't think she can drive."

"Take a cab to the station and wait for the next train. You can send for your luggage later," he said. "That will be five dollars."

I got my mother's purse and gave him the money. He smelled of cigars. And he was out the door.

Maybe it was the five dollars I took from her purse, or maybe the doctor's visit, but after he left she pulled herself up and sat on the edge of the bed.

"I'm not waiting around a train station," she wheezed. "I've got to get away from here."

"But you can't drive!" I cried.

"Put our stuff in the bags," she ordered, laying back down again. Her face was sweating and it was still that funny color.

I threw whatever I saw into the suitcases and shut them.

"Call the bellboy," she rasped.

"But the doctor said—"

She closed her eyes. "Don't argue."

The bellboy somehow got our bags and my mother down into the garage and our car. Barefoot, still in my bathing suit, feeling the salt dry on my legs and back in the clammy air, I followed her into the car.

She switched on the motor and inched out of the garage into the street. Her face was shiny with sweat. I could feel her heat.

Gasping, leaning on the steering wheel, she crawled along the road. Cars honked and passed us. A couple of the drivers glared into our car. A guy on a motorcycle gave us the finger.

She pulled the car over to the curb. "I can't," she wheezed.

I stared at her. Her color was worse. I looked around wildly for help. "I'll get a policeman!"

"No. Stay here," she wheezed. "Drive."

"What?"

"Drive. Get me out of here," she gasped, pulling herself over to the passenger seat where I was sitting.

I got out of the car, ran over to the driver's side and slid behind the wheel as if I were dreaming. My mother collapsed against the door like a rag doll.

I knew enough to start the ignition and press the gas pedal but I wasn't sure about the clutch and gear shift. I turned the key. The car lurched forward and stalled.

"Hold down the clutch," my mother wheezed.

I started the motor again, pushing the clutch with my bare foot. Remembering the gear shift, I pulled it down and pressed the gas pedal. The car galloped forward, scaring me. I jammed on the brake.

"Do it again slower," she gasped.

120

We shot forward like a bat out of hell. And I was driving, my bare foot pressing the accelerator, the engine vibrating up my legs, my wet hands clutching the steering wheel.

"Too fast," she wheezed.

But I kept on going, still in first gear. I was beginning to enjoy myself. I got too close to the curb a couple of times and weaved out into some oncoming cars, but I always jammed my foot on the brake in time, shooting my mother forward and hitting my head on the steering wheel. But crashing the car didn't matter when your only goal was getting your mom where she could breathe. I went through a stop sign as a car suddenly appeared from a side street and hit the horn. The driver looked so frightened I kept my hand down on the honker and we went bellowing along the road scaring everyone out of our way. It was sort of fun but I also hoped all the noise I was making would get a policeman to turn up and take care of my mother because I was only eleven.

I had no idea how far I had driven or for how long, when my mother said, "Pull over. I can drive now."

I looked at her. She was sitting up. Her breathing was quieter and her color better. I pulled over and we jerked to a stop.

She got behind the wheel and drove. It was getting dark. She was breathing now, but she looked exhausted, and when we saw a motel I wanted to stop. Besides, now that I wasn't scared and excited driving I was feeling cold and miserable in my clammy bathing suit— I wished I hadn't left my shirt on the beach. But she wouldn't stop. She needed to put more miles between herself and Atlantic City. "I never want to see that place again," she said, and she kept on driving until we got to East Liverpool.

As soon as we checked into a motel and got into the room, my mother fell asleep on the bed in her clothes.

In the shower, I washed off the sand and salt that was still stuck to me. I wrapped myself in one of the motel towels; it was thin and white and had ROADSIDE MOTEL printed across it in blue letters. When I came into the bedroom my mother was so still on the bed in her clothes I thought she was dead. I put my head down to her mouth. She was breathing. She wasn't dead. I was so relieved I started to cry. I didn't cry when I was so scared in Atlantic City, not even once, but now I couldn't stop, and weeping, choking, my nose and eyes running, I ran into the bathroom and stood hiccupping sobs into my towel.

After a while I came out and sat on my mother's bed. She was still sleeping. I traced my finger along her arm. She didn't wake. I touched her neck, her face. This alive body was my mother, my only parent. Watching her chest move up and down, feeling the warmth of her skin, I realized that only hours ago I could have been touching the flesh of my dead mother. I'd have a dead father, gone forever, and now a dead mother, her body growing stiff and cold. Maybe they would have found each other in the sky. I shivered.

My mother stirred. She was waking. She opened her eyes and stretched. Her color was better, almost normal. "I fell asleep," she said, yawning.

"How do you feel?"

She looked at me and smiled. "Babbie, honey, you did good. You got us out of there." She stood up. "You must be hungry. Put something on and I'll just change this smelly dress."

When we were dressed we went out and got a hamburger.

I had just stashed the photocopies on the shelf behind our hats in the closet when I heard my mother's key in the door. As she came in I saw she wasn't wearing a hat and in the next instant realized my mistake. What if she decides to wear a hat out to dinner? The couch! I could have rolled them under the couch!

She looked at me. "You're home early—didn't you have a show?"

"No," I lied. I had called in sick to go to the library.

She was wearing her brown suit with the brocade trim, white embroidered blouse and high-heeled pumps. I could smell her perfume. She always wore too much. "Traffic was terrible," she sighed, dropping on the couch, slipping off her shoes. She looked at me. "Shouldn't you be getting ready?"

"Ready for what?"

"I thought you had a date with Nate."

I had completely forgotten it. But I couldn't leave her alone with my father in the closet. I looked at my watch and hurried to the phone.

Nate wasn't home yet, so I left a message with his mother. "I may be coming down with something," I told her.

Pleased, my mother asked me to go to dinner with her.

I shook my head. I had to get rid of her. I had to find another hiding place. I had to protect her from her own story.

"Just to the deli?" she asked.

"What if I run into Nate? Or someone who knows him?"

She sighed. "Well, maybe we'll just open up some soup or something," she said, getting up.

"But I don't want soup!" I said, following her into the kitchen. "I'm starved! Bring me a sandwich from the deli?"

She looked doubtfully out the window. "It's starting to rain."

"I'm hungry," I whined.

She turned to me. "Babbie, you don't always have to eat like a horse, you know."

"Please?"

"Okay, okay," she said, heading to the bedroom.

"Where are you going?" I yelled.

She turned to me, amused. "I'm just getting my hat."

"You'll mess up your hair!"

She stopped and patted her head. "You think so?" she said, sighing. "So what do you want?" she asked, pulling on her coat.

"Corned beef! A corned beef sandwich! And potato salad! Hurry!"

She turned to me. "Babbie, are you all right?"

"Yes! Sure! I'm hungry!"

"Be right back," she said, as she left.

I jumped up and hurried into the bedroom. Reaching up for the photocopies I heard her key in the door.

"Came back for the umbrella," she called.

I waited in the bedroom until I heard her leave again. Then I climbed up on a chair in the kitchen and found a hollowed out niche over the cupboard. The copies just fit.

Thirteen

"THIS SUNDAY'S FATHER'S DAY," Dr. Herman says.

"That lets me out."

"Go on," he says.

"That's it. End of story."

"You know, you haven't mentioned your father since the day you told me about the murders."

"So?"

"So I wonder about that."

"There's nothing more to say."

"You have no memory of him? Nothing?"

"Nothing."

"Well, growing up you must have missed having a father," he says.

"You can't miss what you never had." I don't know why I lied. Shame, maybe, even in here. But it didn't feel like that. It felt more like fear. Or my mother holding her hand over my mouth.

"You didn't spring full blown from the forehead of Zeus, you know. You did have a father."

"No, I didn't," I say. "He's a void, a vacuum. He's a newspaper story."

Dr. Herman clears his throat and I hear him stir in his chair. "You were two years old when he was killed, and one of the most important stages of human development is the time before speech—especially if there was trauma. Without language, overpowering feelings can't be understood or sorted out. They go underground and lie there festering."

I don't answer. His words dredge up a night several months ago that I thought I'd put out of my mind.

"What are you thinking?" he prompts.

"About something that happened," I finally say.

"Tell me about it."

I press my lips together.

"You know," he says, "when you're reluctant to talk about something in here, I suspect its importance."

"I don't want you to know what a wimp I am," I say.

"Go on," he says.

"I went in!" I say in a rush. "I went into that terrible place. Dark. It was dark. It smelled of death. It was awful—" I cover my wet face. I cannot go on.

He waits.

"And I let him," I finally whisper.

"Let him what?" he says, handing me the Kleenex.

I wipe my eyes and blow my nose. "I let him take me in there."

"In where? Start at the beginning," he says

"It was a night, oh, four, five months ago. Nate and I had gone out for dinner, and on the way home he parked in front of this bar. It was dark and at first I didn't know where we were. And then I saw. It was a saloon the Lonardo family owns—a son or nephew or someone. Everyone knows they own it. Nate got out of the car, came around and opened my door. You're coming in, he said. I told him no. I told him I didn't want to. He grabbed my arm. He was smiling, saying something like I was being ridiculous, making too much of it, these were just Lonardo's relatives, something like that. And I thought, yeah, he's probably right. So I got out of the car." I stop, breathing as if I'd been running.

"Then what?" Dr. Herman finally asks.

"The place was dark, and so quiet it was eerie. There was a long wooden bar along the wall. A few men were scattered on the stools. No one was talking or looking at the TV over the bar or even moving; they could have been sitting up dead. The place smelled of beer and bodies; it smelled of decay. Nate grabbed my arm and took me to a leather booth in the back. There was an awful silence in the place. It rang in my ears. We sat down. A waiter came over. I wanted to scream but I ordered a scotch and soda." I couldn't seem to get my breath.

Dr. Herman waits. Then he says, "Go on."

"The light in the bar was red, I guess from the neon sign outside, but it was like reflecting the fires of hades, like Nate had dragged me down to hell. I looked up and my mind flooded with an image of Lonardo and his henchmen driving away in the Peerless, my father and uncle bleeding on the ground."

"What did you do?"

"Do? I drank my scotch and soda, and ordered another one. I told you I was a wimp."

"No," he says. "Not a wimp. Confused. Alone. Trying to overcome the lifelong problem of your father. Subjected to cruelty from your husband. But hardly a wimp."

"You don't think so?"

"On the contrary. I think you're brave."

"You do?"

"Yes, I do." He clears his throat. "See you tomorrow."

At home I pull into the circular driveway. The house is set well back from the street, an imposing structure of fifteen rooms, surrounded by Nate's emerald green lawn, fragrant dogwoods, azaleas, the English ivy that clings gracefully to the facade. A bay window curves and defines the dining room. Gazing at the house I remember the day Nate announced that he had bought it, a place I had never seen. I realize that I have arrived at his home, not mine.

Inside, I greet Maddie, my housekeeper, in her good-smelling kitchen. Fragrant pot roast with carrots and potatoes are in the oven; an apple pie stands cooling on the counter, its delicious aroma lifting into the room. I hear the shouts of my children as they play outside on the patio; they are forbidden by their father to play on the perfect velvety lawn. The table is set with napkins, a white damask cloth, blue-and-white bone china. Wedgwood. Even our everyday dishes are the best, but I think with an odd pang of nostalgia of the mismatched cracked plates and jelly jars my mother, Kenny and I used in my former screwed-up life. I smile at Maddie, ask for telephone messages. I am an impostor. On my way upstairs I hear my husband's voice on the telephone, and stop, panicked, as if I don't know my next lines for the part I'm supposed to play.

I bathe the children. I hear my husband's step on the stair. Why does my heart drop at the sound? After all, he has never hit me. Never. Oh, once he shoved me against the wall, and there was the time he pushed me out of a moving car, but it wasn't going very fast. I have no black eyes or bruised flesh or broken bones to show; I can't say, See? Look what he did! To myself. To anyone. Bones and flesh heal but my invisible wounds fester secretly.

We don't fight. I agree it is my fault that the baby doesn't stop crying, that his friend Jack dies suddenly at 45, that the rain spoils his golf game, that I spend too much money at the supermarket, that Lewis has the measles, that his sales manager left, that the dealer down the street sold more cars this month. He comes home with these frustrations and disappointments and directs his anger at me as if I am responsible and although I know better, I concur.

He comes into the bedroom where I am reading to the children and greets me absentmindedly, a peck on the cheek. Although Nate showers twice a day, he has begun to smell sort of rank to me, as if meanness has an odor in the air, the stink percolating up from his pores. I feel him staring at me and look up to see his face broaden, thicken, his eyes turn heavy lidded. I see the face of Lonardo.

He sits down at the desk and opens his mail.

I am a woman with a rich husband who says he loves me, a cook and a maid and a big beautiful house. I try to please him and I fail. I take care of my children. I have a busy social life and many friends. So what does it matter if I'm impersonating myself? What does it matter that it exhausts me? I am raising my children and do not mind that the sound of my husband's foot on the stair fills me with such a feeling of dread that a near traffic accident while driving, a visit to a terminally sick friend in the hospital, the sound of footsteps behind me on a dark street, remind me of Nathan Hoffman.

Maddie calls us down to dinner.

Fourteen

AFTER MY MOTHER went to bed that night I took the newspaper photocopies down and spread them out on the kitchen table. The room still smelled of the corned beef sandwiches we'd had for dinner. The thick paper made such a loud crackling sound, I tip-toed to her door. Silence. I waited, listening, but heard nothing and sat down with the *Cleveland Plain Dealer*.

It was as if I was in the Chicago of the bloody bootlegging wars. But this was Cleveland: a place of tall stalks of August corn, orchards of autumn apples, picture-book red barns. Trolleys and bakeries with the aroma of baklava and strudel drifting into the street. Bowling alleys, Dairy Queens, miles of old shaded streets. Families leading safe, ordinary lives with mundane problems: a lost job, an illness or auto accident, a grandparent's quiet death. Staring at the headlines in front of me I am jealous, ashamed, proud:

ROSEN'S BABY COOS AS WIDOW TELLS OF DOUBLE MURDER

CROWDS ATTEND ROSEN'S FUNERAL

FURTHER DETAILS OF MURDERS

SYNDICATES FIGHT ALCOHOL BATTLE

U.S. AGENTS REVEAL WAR OVER "B-39"

Reading the articles, reading between the lines, the tale comes to me like an ongoing dream . . . .

Lou had left his family's bakery and developed a prosperous bootlegging business with a partner, a Mr. Gross (who prudently disappeared after the murders leaving no trace—not even a first name). They bought second class alcohol from smugglers in New York who bribed freight agents and shipped it in boxes labeled "furniture." Lou then sold it to gin mills in Cleveland, where it was refined, flavored with anise and sold as gin. Known as "B-39," the alcohol was poisonous in the raw but could be refined in ten minutes by passing it into one small still and out another.

He moved through his short life with heartbreaking ease. Wasn't selling bootleg whiskey better than rising in the middle of the night to bake bread in hot ovens? Better than living with a demanding father, overworked mother and eight siblings and step-siblings? The workday at Rosen's Bakery began at three in the morning and didn't end until nine at night. Bread, rolls and pastries had to be baked; ovens, floors and display cases scrubbed; deliveries made to grocery stores and restaurants throughout the city in a horse and wagon; customers waited on; books kept. Lou was sickened by the monotony, the meager wages, the long hours, the oven's heat. Already a school dropout, he often ran away from home, whored and gambled and skimmed money from the cash register. The sons of hardworking Jewish immigrants became doctors, comedians, merchants or gangsters, and when Prohibition was enacted into law, Lou found the career he was born to.

One day as he played pinochle with his cronies in the back room of Peter Tabac's cigar shop, Joe Lonardo lumbered in. Better known as Big Joe, he was six feet two inches tall, weighed almost 300 pounds, had a blind eye, drooping eyelids, and dominated Cleveland's world of crime, politics and government.

"Louie," Lonardo said, pulling up a chair. "I think you should get back in the bakery business."

"Not interested," Lou replied. Or something of the sort. In any case, he declined. Obviously.

"Don't be stupid. We'll get your B-39 anyway."

Lou looked up from his cards. "And how do you propose to do that?"

"How do you think?" Lonardo said.

"You hijack me, I'll hijack you."

"Then we'll get you," Lonardo said through the cigar in his mouth as the three other players at the table studied their cards and pretended not to hear. "Count on it," he said softly as he got up and lumbered out the door.

Two weeks later Lonardo hijacked 25 drums of alcohol from Lou's warehouse at gunpoint. A week later Lou paid off the night watchman at a railroad yard and helped himself to Lonardo's alcohol.

Isn't there something erotic and heroic about standing up to the Mafia? Did my mother become a bootlegger's wife to fill the gap left by an orphaned, unnurtured childhood? A gap so large only a man of daring and danger could fill it? When my girlfriends told me about the moans and squeaking mattress behind their parents' bedroom door, I always felt a stab of relief, pretending that my widowed mother didn't do *that*. But now, reading, I imagined her excitement over his reckless defiance. She had grown up, after all, within the dead heart of a nineteenth century Dickensian orphanage, as cloistered and preoccupied with sin as a nun, a place where if a boy was caught talking to a girl he was taken downstairs and beaten by the bigger boys, a place where she was never touched or held or hugged and so unloved she would have surely been doomed to a life of virginity if it weren't such a challenge to my wild, carnal father to capture and possess this prim, skittish eighteen-year-old with her cool, immaculate life of the mind. Is that how they managed the leap to each other?

But her brainy innocence and her books, where passion is safely confined to the page, must have intimidated and infuriated Lou, because—the story goes— one day, several months after they were married, he found her reading while the kitchen sink was piled with dirty dishes.

"I'm going out," he told her, "and if all these dishes aren't washed by the time I come back I swear to God I'll smash every last one of them."

He had bought her diamonds and oriental rugs and a piano that no one could play, and he therefore expected her to do his bidding. But either forgetting his orders or defying them, she kept on reading.

He came home an hour and a half later, and true to his word, smashed every dirty dish, one at a time, against the wall.

I have no idea if the story is true or false. I relate it as it came down to me from Uncle Sid and Uncle Marvin, no doubt embellished in the tellings, my uncles shiny-eyed and vicariously thrilled at such violence so nicely distanced from their own safe lives. Another legend has it that in a traffic argument with a streetcar conductor, Lou got out of his car, pulled the conductor down from his perch by his tie and knocked him flat. This story has the note of authenticity since it was told to me by my brother, who was there, sitting in the passenger seat.

And then there was the time Lou killed a striker who was picketing Rosen's Bakery. That story is coolly verified right here in the newspaper in front of me:

ROSEN ONCE SENT UP AFTER KILLING. REVENGE THEORY IN MURDER BASED ON LABOR FIGHT.

The theory that revenge might have prompted the murder of Louis Rosen arose from the fact that the Rosen family was involved in labor troubles, during which Joe Feld, a picket, was killed.

According to records in the County prosecutor's office, Feld grabbed the bread from a woman coming out of Rosen's bakery at 2535 Woodland Ave. S.E. Louis Rosen, his brother, their father, and an employee ran from the bakery and a fight ensued. Louis, according to the records, admitted striking Feld with his fist. The coroner reported Feld had been struck on the head with a piece of pipe.

Louis and his brother were bound over to the grand jury on charges of second degree murder, and the father and the employee were bound over on manslaughter charges. The grand jury exonerated the latter two but returned indictments against the brothers who were found guilty, however, only of assault and battery.

Louis was fined $200 and sentenced to four months in the workhouse and his brother was fined $25 and costs.

The feeling against the Rosen family among Feld's friends was so strong that in 1921 police were called to quell a riot at the funeral of Louis Rosen's father. According to police a number of persons attempted to stone the casket.

"Listen," my uncle Marvin said to me after he became wealthy with a chain of bakeries, "Your dad was just unlucky. Look at Bugsy Siegel and Legs Diamond. Al Capone. Dutch Schultz. They're still writing books and making movies about those guys. And what about O'Hare for God's sake, getting the biggest airport in the world named after him. A bootlegger's son! How do you think Joe Kennedy got started? And the Bronfmans up in Canada with Seagrams? Bootlegging!" Uncle Marvin shook his head. "Your dad was just unlucky," he said again.

In long-festering rationalization and guilt, my father's sisters, Sally and Milly, and brothers Marvin and Manny, had put out a kind of revisionist story.

Blame was everywhere and nowhere; everyone pointed a finger at everyone else. His wife should have made him stop bootlegging . . . . His brother should have kept him working in the bakery . . . . His father shouldn't have been so tough on him . . . . His mother should have been more affectionate . . . . His partner should have . . . . His sisters should have . . . . His friends should have . . . .

I imagined the finger pointed at me, too. Two years old, wetting my bed and spitting up my bottle, I was already responsible for two murders. If I had been as lovable as the babies of unmurdered fathers, he wouldn't have risked his life playing chicken with the Mafia. He would have wanted to stay in the bakery business and stay alive to be my daddy.

The fingers all finally turned and pointed to my mother. It was her fault. She should have kept him home that night. She shouldn't have had her nose in a book all the time, who did she think she was? She shouldn't have spent so much money on that house, those clothes. She shouldn't have played those scratchy operas on the phonograph—no wonder he was out all the time. She should have been a better wife, mother, person.

But no one pointed a finger at Lou. By virtue of being dead he was blameless, his guilt buried six feet under, leaving the survivors to play musical chairs of blame. I used to imagine him looking down from heaven or up from hell saying with his famous charm, Listen, all I did was give the folks what they want, supply and demand, what could be more American? Who do you think were my best customers? Judges and cops, teachers and doctors and all the other pillars of society. Besides, he'd say, nobody was so upset when I was bringing in the money.

Years later, when I finally visited the cemetery in Cleveland where he was buried, I pointed my finger at his grave. It was his fault.

The woman in the office of Park Synagogue Cemetery had looked up the site of his grave in a big dusty book, turning faded pages of neatly hand-written names of the long dead. Then she drew a circle around his grave site on a xeroxed map and handed it to me. It was the first tangible evidence I'd ever had of his existence and taking the map from her hand felt like a subversive act.

As I left the office, the glare from the sun was sharp on the tombstones, the air still as the dead. I wandered among the graves with the map looking for my father. It was an old crowded cemetery with the dead buried close together, laid out side by side, head to head, foot to foot, the tombstones reaching as far as the eye could see into the horizon. Finally a greenskeeper going by in his truck stopped to help me. I showed him the map, he pointed, and drove off. And there it was, ten feet from where I was standing.

"Louis Rosen" the tombstone read, **"Your Memory Is Dear."** I wondered who ordered that lie; surely not my mother who tried all her life to obliterate it. The word **"FATHER"** stood proudly at the top of the marker in huge letters. *Father*! Another lie written in stone.

I stood trying to imagine the burial all those years ago. My mother's collapse that day. Kenny reciting the Kaddish in his six-year-old voice. Lou's weeping siblings. The bootleggers in their dark suits and fedoras. The murderer, Lonardo. The detectives. The carpet of flowers on his casket. The crowds kept at a respectful distance by the police. I wept as if I had been there that day, as if I were finally burying him. My eyes and nose running, I mopped up my face and looked around in embarrassment. No one was there. Anyway, it was okay to cry in the cemetery. You were supposed to cry in the cemetery, and for a moment I felt part of the shared universe of daughters grieving for their fathers.

His dead neighbors were in well-kept graves, but my father's lay in black-sheep neglect, sunken and over-grown with weeds. I walked back to the office to arrange for the grave's repair and perpetual care. But I didn't go in. I didn't want to. It was too late to have a father. He was nothing to me or too much to me and I got in my car and left.

I looked up at the clock in surprise. It was after midnight and I hadn't finished reading through the pile of news-papers. But I had to be at May's at nine the next morning for a noon fashion show and reluctantly rolled them up in their rubber bands, climbed up to their hiding place and stashed them away.

My mother was waiting for me when I got home from work the next evening and we went to Goldman's Deli for dinner. Sometimes we'd go to Mills Cafeteria, or a nearby diner, or Wong's for Chinese. But we never ate at home. Never. Once when I was sick and my mother brought me a steaming bowl of chicken soup in bed I thought I must be on my death bed. Amazed that the soup was so delicious, I asked her who made it. But she didn't get mad, further proof that I was dying. All she said was, "I did," with great dignity.

The deli smelled of corned beef and pickles. After sitting down and ordering, my mother started talking about something. Half listening, I started to wonder if she loved my father. Or if she wished with all her heart that she'd never laid eyes on him. Or was she so crazy in love she couldn't bear to speak of her broken heart? I wanted to know.

I remembered the story Kenny told me about how as a bachelor Uncle Marvin once covered for our father when someone saw him with another woman. The story goes that he insisted to my mother that the tattletale was mistaken, that it was he, Marvin, and not Lou she saw with the woman. I wondered if my mother believed him. I wondered about his temper, too. Did he beat her? But I couldn't make myself ask.

She talked and talked all through dinner, burying her secrets under a torrent of words. As usual. There didn't seem room enough in her head and her mouth for all she had to say. Her favorite subjects were politics, the weather, books, and moral choice. She talked about Sinclair Lewis. Fitzgerald. Edna Ferber. Kafka. Also communism and capitalism. Socialism. Suffrage. The New Deal. She pontificated on courage and independence and spoke like an aristocrat about taste in art, literature, clothes, life.

Reading everything, remembering everything she read, she would tell you more than you wanted to know about anarchy. About the League of Nations. John L. Lewis and Leon Trotsky. How Roosevelt's NRA and WPA saved the nation. She loved getting into political arguments with people because her head was stuffed with esoteric minutiae just waiting to spring on some poor Republican. Who would soon find himself hopelessly outmatched by her facts, her passion, her verbosity.

She also lectured me grandly on the virtues Dr. Wolfenstein drummed into her head for twelve years. In the Home, once a week the children were assembled in the Prayer Hall on the top floor of the schoolhouse for one of his lectures on personal morality, integrity, uprightness, virtue, and the ten commandments. Determined to shape his charges' minds and characters toward a moral, ethical and honorable life, he told them to be truthful and honest, obey laws and rules, honor the elderly, love and respect their parents, resist temptations, be good citizens and patriots, keep their promises, control their temper, love their neighbors, refrain from jealousy and envy, work hard, trust God and stay close to Him, be modest and humble, be grateful and appreciative, love the president of the country, be good and righteous, respect their teachers, plan for the future, help those in need, be kind and obedient, be happy and strive to make others happy, meet troubles and hardship with a strong mind, be faithful to the Jewish religion by observing its laws and history, love all children alike without showing favoritism, atone for their sins and be anxious to improve.

I know she took it all in because she taught me everything she learned. But no matter how much she preached, I saw her ultimate rejection and contempt for every one of Wolfenstein's revered institutions—marriage, religion, politics, formal education, medicine, law, government.

Taught religion, she became an agnostic; taught truthfulness, she lied; taught humility and gratitude for an orphan's room and board, she developed a ferocious pride. Instructed on modesty in dress and behavior, she exchanged her scratchy uniform for the glittering dresses she loved and spent her widow years before the Crash as the quintessential flapper. All of which reliably added yet another layer of confusion into my already confused life. Do what I say, not what I do, she told me.

"More coffee?" the waitress asked, holding the carafe aloft.

"No thanks," I said. I was still eating, but it was as if my mother had inhaled the roast chicken, mashed potatoes and string beans—only a neat pile of picked-clean bones was left on her plate. She always ate like that. Before meals she'd get uncharacteristically quiet, her silence so deep it seemed to have a weight. Her breath would come faster, her hairline get moist; sometimes she'd start to wheeze. Then when the food came, she'd eat with one arm circled around her plate as if it was about to be snatched away.

In the orphanage, she climbed over the eight-foot fence to steal food from nearby grocers or neighbors' kitchens. At mealtimes, five hundred hungry orphans sat at ten long tables in enforced silence. The food was boiled in huge vats. Breakfast was a kind of gruel the children called mush, weak coffee and a slice of stale bread thinly covered with margarine. Dinner was a stringy stew or green pea hash. Her twelve years in the Home must have left her so famished for so long that it didn't feel like hunger, only a vast, incomprehensible inner vacuum that could have been confused with the absence of love.

"Let's have dessert," my mother said.

Anxious to get back to my reading, I shook my head.

"Well, I can't resist," she said.

She ordered apple pie with vanilla ice cream and coffee. "Did you know that Dostoyevsky started out as a socialist?" She asked me.

"What?"

"When you read *Crime And Punishment* it's hard to believe, isn't it? The book's so full of his hatred of revolutionaries."

"Well . . . ."

"But he did. He was a committed socialist. When he was 27, Czar Nicholas had him arrested as a revolutionary conspirator. Sentenced him to eight years forced labor. Do you know what changed him?"

"No, I . . . ."

"He had always idolized the peasants of Russia. But when he was thrown into prison with them he found out what they were *really* like. And he despised them! I'll tell you something, Babbie, you really can't blame him—I understand how he felt. It's one thing to be for the downtrodden, the peasants. But I imagine that actually living with them must be quite another matter," she said, lifting her prideful chin as if she had never heard of the Jewish Orphan Home.

The only time my mother was quiet was when she was reading, or when Franklin Roosevelt was on the radio. Listening raptly, she nodded in agreement and smiled as if he was in the room with her. Sometimes she closed her eyes and swayed a little like a person listening to music. Hanging on his every word as his melodious disembodied voice floated from the mesh front of our console radio, he was father, husband, brother; he was everyone she never had. He was salvation. He would save the country. Us. *Her*.

It had begun raining and a gray-haired couple came into the deli shaking out their umbrella. They hung it on the coat rack and sat down at a table on the other side of the restaurant.

Finished at last, my mother looked at the check that had been waiting and put the money down. Then she walked over to the coat rack, lifted the couple's umbrella from its hook and walked out of the restaurant with it.

I followed her outside. She was standing under the umbrella waiting for me.

"You took their umbrella!" I cried.

She looked at me. "It was raining."

I stood staring, getting soaked. Then I got under the umbrella with her and we went home.

Fifteen

WHEN I THOUGHT my mother was safely asleep that night I climbed up to my hiding place to retrieve the papers. And returned to the tale . . . .

One day Lou heard through an informer that Lonardo had put out a contract on his life. Now he had to take Lonardo's threat seriously. Now he didn't dare leave his house. He paced. He peeked through the closed curtains. Jumped when the doorbell rang. Snapped at my mother. Called his friends in the trade at odd hours pestering them for information about Lonardo and his henchmen. As if it could save him.

Meanwhile, my mother's sister, Della, her husband, Adolph—Addie—Adelson, and their seven-month-old baby, Lucille, arrived from their home in Philadelphia for a visit. It was Della's first trip to her hometown since her marriage two years earlier.

My mother had invited some of Della's old friends to dinner for the following evening and the guests, three or four couples, began arriving at seven-thirty. After the roast beef (or perhaps chicken—in those days chicken was a delicacy), baked potatoes, asparagus, and German chocolate cake, Lou set up card tables for bridge, declining in his restlessness to play. As the guests settled down at the tables, he paced, disappeared upstairs, came down, paced again, offered drinks, soft drinks probably, annoyed the bridge players with his kibitzing, and finally, to everyone's relief, went back upstairs.

"That's rubber," someone finally said, getting up, stretching. As if signaled, the other guests began pushing their chairs back, getting into their coats, offering thanks. It had been a pleasant evening, and chattering, everyone left with smiles and hollered good nights from the quiet street.

Addie was gathering up the cards from the bridge tables as Lou came pounding down the steps. "Come on, Addie, let's go," he said. Restless, sick of being confined to the house all these days and nights, he grabbed his coat and looked at his brother-in-law. "Come on," he said, again. "Let's play a little pinochle, see some of the boys." If he wasn't alone, surely a short ride over to Tabac's cigar store would be okay. Or so he thought.

Aunt Della and my mother were collecting the coffee cups scattered around the room and Addie may have looked over at his wife for permission. Or perhaps not. Perhaps he wouldn't do that in front of his macho brother-in-law, and he may have avoided eye contact with her as he put on his coat. Maybe my mother, who certainly knew about the contract on Lou's life, tried to stop them. Or maybe she didn't. Maybe she was tired of having him home all the time, pacing and snapping at her. Maybe it was guilt from her silence that night that sealed her lips all these years.

In any case we know that Lou took Addie out with him into Lonardo's night. It was November so there could have been the lingering scent of burning leaves in the crisp air and a brilliant umbrella of stars overhead lighting up the driveway.

An hour later Lou's partner, Mr. Gross, dashed into the back room of Tabac's cigar shop. Peter Tabac was sitting alone at the card table playing solitaire.

"Where's everybody!" Gross yelled.

"They left," Tabac said, without looking up from his cards.

"Lou too? Lou left?" Gross cried, looking around wildly.

"Yeah."

"I've got to reach him!"

"So call him at home."

"No! Before! Before he gets home!" Gross hollered. "When did he leave!"

"Ten, fifteen minutes," Tabac said, as Gross dashed out again.

He must have driven to the house, heard the shots and kept on going, prudently vanishing forever. Della and my mother heard the shots, too. Della in her innocence may have thought they were nothing more than an engine backfiring, but my mother knew better, ran to the window in terror and saw the two bleeding bodies in the driveway. Screaming, she ran outside, followed by Della. Two or three neighbors came running and pulled the sisters in their bloody nightgowns off their husbands' bodies as their howls reached the star-lit sky in a grotesque duet of high C's. My mother began babbling gibberish, frightening the neighbors. No one went to the crying children who were awakened by the commotion. Or perhaps they—we—were quiet, stunned and terrified by our mothers' screams into an unnatural, unblinking, silence.

Lou and Addie lay in the driveway, still bleeding, Lou from a sawed off shotgun blast through his heart, Addie from two 32-caliber bullets through his throat and head, both bodies brutally slashed, cut down in the moment of their blatant confidence in themselves—their blood thick and fast; their muscles tight and hard; their groins ready at a moment's erotic memory or thought or flashing sight of some random feminine leg or nape of neck; their futures untested and their minds full of the grand dreams of youth. Now, shot and slashed to death they were frozen in their heyday, the humiliation and transparency of growing old transcended, to be passed in age by their own children.

They had fought bitterly, valiantly. Stabbed, slashed, bleeding, they got up again and again, fighting back, arm wrestling the killers for the knives, dodging, ducking, side-stepping in a macabre ballet of death. Finally, still alive, they had to be shot. Subdued at last, dead at last, the sudden silence was so powerful it seemed to paralyze the earth's rotation.

And the universe was changed forever with the force of myth, as if there were no other history that mattered. What conceit! What pomposity! But that's the way it was in our family; the egotism and bravado of secrets, grief and guilt.

Reading, I did a double take. Shit! There's Gross safe in his car while my father's getting killed! Sitting there on his ass! Some partner! Gross *knew* it was a trap, he knew they were waiting to kill him, why the hell didn't he get there in time! Or use the goddamn telephone? My God, I was two years old and *I* could have made it. All the asshole had to do was get there a couple of minutes sooner. A couple of minutes! That's all! My father and Addie would be alive. The goddamn coward was thinking of his own goddamn yellow neck. Driving slow, playing it safe. I wish to hell Kenny and I had been older. We would have got there. I hope Gross is dead. I hope he suffered, I hope he took a long time to die. Lucky for him I don't know where he is or I swear to God I'd kill him myself.

After I calmed down I wondered what our lives would have been like if Gross had actually made it in time. Lou could have wound up in Las Vegas, rich and safe, my mother free of her guilt and silence and delusions, wrapped in clothes and jewels, surrounded by the books she loved. Kenny would run the casino, and I'd be a croupier with swift skillful hands, leaning over the chips, showing off my cleavage, my father's daughter. Or I'd book the shows and run the restaurants. Our dad would wear beautiful suits and smoke cigars in a grand office; people would do his bidding. Maybe I could be proud of my father in a place like that instead of the shiver of shame I felt now, sitting here with his story.

Or he could have gone straight, couldn't he? After all, he was only 29. But the stories of his violent temper and lust and foolish daring just didn't fit the stoic, steady life of a baker. More likely, whether he went out that night or not, his fantasy of being invincible and invisible to his enemies would have escalated his war with the Mafia until he got killed. Or killed someone, and got caught and sent to jail. Or the Chair. Or not got caught and become involved in even bigger and more dangerous escapades. Feeling a pang of guilt I thought our lives could have been worse if he had lived. But of course I'll never know, and when I tried to imagine what could have happened it turned us all into people I did not recognize.

Years later I recognized the name of my father's killer when his son, Angelo, turned Federal informant and testified in a New York mobster's trial. Reading about Angelo Lonardo's testimony in the newspaper, staring at his picture, all I felt was a mild curiosity at the odd parallel of our lives. Angelo had murdered the murderer of *his* father, Big Joe Lonardo, who was the murderer of *my* father. I had not fantasized about revenge. It wasn't like in the movies where the hero searches for his father's killer but when his long-sought target is finally at his mercy, staring into his gun, pleading for his life, he puts his gun back in his holster and walks away. You've seen that movie a hundred times.

My mother had already obliterated my father's life and death leaving me feeling only a sad and confusing gap. And when I was old enough to seek him out I found only stories and old newspapers. And that it was too late for dreams of revenge.

The address of the murder scene was in one of the newspaper articles. At dawn, before my mother woke, I drove over to the house and parked across the street. The place looked familiar and yet dreamlike, a brick two-story, like millions of other brick two-stories, smaller than I had expected. How could such violence occur in this ordinary cliche of a house? And why was my heart hammering like this?

I decided to get a closer look and got out of the car. The morning air felt young and fresh and the early light was dappled through the budding May trees. Standing in the driveway, I smelled the faintly sweet aroma of an apple tree in the yard. Was it there that night? And is this where the bodies were sprawled? I wanted to drop to my knees; I wanted to feel what they felt of the hard ground, the rough asphalt. But I stood erect feeling a strange thrill and then, from nowhere, from somewhere, the threat of tears in my throat. I wanted a headstone, a marker, an acknowledgement of his life where I stood, but the ground was barren, innocent of even a faded bloodstain; once again the truth made invisible, unimaginable. Erased. Not worth mentioning.

But not that night. I was told how people gathered on the sidewalk and drove by the house, slowly, bumper to bumper, craning their necks to gawk. Why this fascination with someone else's horror? Relief that it's not them? Or is there an excitement, a carnal, lecherous thrill to violence? Well, don't I feel it? Am I not standing here gawking at my own history?

I wanted to see inside the house. I stood listening. It was quiet. If I'm caught I'll just say I'm sorry, I used to live here. I pressed my nose against one of the windows. It was dark inside but I could make out a living room. Is that where they all played bridge that night? I imagined my father alive in that house, sleeping upstairs in his pajamas, being a husband, a dad, a brother. Eating roasted chicken and German chocolate cake and kibitzing the bridge game that night. I walked around to the other windows and peered at the kitchen, the dining room. Chairs, lamps, tables. A couch. I didn't know what I had expected to find by sneaking out of the apartment at five in the morning and peeping into windows, but it wasn't this banal, ordinary house. It didn't fit. It belonged in someone else's life.

Where was the large proud home I had imagined? The grand piano and oriental rugs, the velvets and brocades I had been told about? The extravagant draperies? Kenny had told me about his wonderful miniature car and elaborate toys, and hadn't I seen my mother's diamonds with my own eyes before they went for Kenny's college tuition? Was it all some kind of strange illusion or dream? Or is this? I saw a light go on in an upstairs window. Then in the kitchen. They were getting up.

The sky had become mottled with gray clouds threatening rain and a brisk wind came up, chilling me. I heard a murmur of voices coming from the kitchen and ran back to the car like a thief caught with someone else's life. I sat watching the house come alive with lights and movement—I thought I heard a child's voice. Well, other people live here now. I have no claim. I needed to get away from this place. From my father's life and death. From his hold on me. He was gone. It was over. And good riddance.

I started the car and headed home. It was fully light now, cars began filling the streets, the city was waking. When I got home I parked the car, climbed the steps and unlocked the door to our apartment. I had made it back in time. My mother wasn't up yet.

I got undressed and went back to bed. I was tired. I was tired of trying to bury my father. I was tired of the secrets. I was tired of my own imaginings. Of the newspapers that were rolled up in their hiding place. Seeing the house had left me feeling no better and no worse;

only an odd letdown, as if I had gotten rid of something I would miss. All I wanted now was the kind of life that would fit into the simple brick dwelling I had just left.

Sixteen

"DON'T BE SOMEBODY'S wife," my mother said. "Look at Mary Lou Baxter, already set up in a grand apartment on Park Avenue in Manhattan." Mary Lou had been a model with me at Halle's before leaving for New York and sexual success. "Be an adventuress," she told me. "Use them before they use you."

So of course I got married just as soon as I turned nineteen. I was afraid if I didn't get away I would stay with her forever, my mother's handmaiden, mesmerized by her will, her torrents of words. We would become one of those pathetic mother-daughter duets, both of us growing old in a dim, sour-smelling apartment, eating lunch in tearooms, driving to national parks for vacations like two old maids, while I withered away helplessly in her grip. Kenny had left. The good jobs and the men were gone. I was all she had and she clung to me with the desperation and determination of a woman drowning in her own destiny. As if I could rescue her.

I had enough trouble trying to rescue myself. Uneducated, achingly young, trained only for sexual adventure, I had maybe $35, and no skills except the modeling I hated. To escape, I figured I needed a weight to counterbalance my mother's insatiable needs. I needed an institution. The institution of marriage.

I met Nate when I was seventeen, out of school and modeling downtown. He drove up on our first date, handsome in gray slacks and a blue sweater, the son of a well-known prosperous businessman, a catch. He was 24, living with his parents and working in his father's Chrysler agency. Already balding, he had a broad face, heavy brows and thin lips—I thought he looked like Lawrence Olivier. He drove a thrilling red convertible and took me to dances at the Mentor On The Lake Pavilion, to the Hotel Statler for dinners, to parties, to the movies. I loved riding at his side with the top down and my hair blowing; I loved his swagger; I loved when we parked at Shaker Lakes and necked; I loved my erotic awakening. Nate was Prince Charming in a red convertible come to save me.

His hobby was photography. One day after we had been dating for a few months, we went to his basement darkroom so I could watch him print some pictures he had taken of me. He had posed me outdoors among a cluster of the white birch trees he liked, and at the beach sitting in the surf with the waves lapping up over me. We stood watching his enlarged 8-by-10 idea of me float up in the printing solution, a nice Jewish girl who had the good manners not to look Jewish. His mother wore tight clothes in shiny fabrics and jangling jewelry, but he wanted me to wear Peter Pan collars, tweed suits, and sweater sets like the gentile women who lived on Chesterland estates and kept horses. After we were married he bought me a ski jacket for one of my birthdays (I didn't know how to ski) and a sewing machine for another. I didn't know how to sew, either.

"Nate, is that you?" his mother called from upstairs.

He kept on moving the pictures around in the developer with a clothes pin as if he hadn't heard her.

"Nate?" she called again. "Are you down there?"

Still, he didn't answer. "Your mother's calling you," I finally said, surprised at the way he ignored her.

"I'm busy!" he yelled.

"Nate, honey . . . ."

"Stop calling me! I told you I'm busy!"

"But I . . . ."

"Ma, Shut *up*! I'm working!"

I couldn't believe my ears. I had never heard anyone speak to their mother like that. It appalled me. It excited me. I stared at him in the amber safe-light. He looked undaunted, bold. Here was a man who could save me from my mother. I fell madly in love on the spot.

And later, when I met his family, I was irrevocably hooked. Especially by his mother. Becky was one of those cooking, hovering, self-sacrificing Jewish mothers I had always coveted. Although I observed that Nate's father, Morris, treated her with the same contempt as Nate did, it didn't occur to me to worry that Morris was a dangerous role model for my future husband. I was getting a real family. I loved their large, comfortable house. The Sabbath dinners. The warm tumult of aunts and uncles and cousins in back yard picnics. *Yom Kippur* and Passover dinners with ritual foods on immaculate linen. And the food, the food— matzo ball soup, chopped liver, gefilte fish, brisket in brown gravy, roasted chicken, potato *latkes*, noodle *kugel*, sponge cake, brownies, chocolate chip cookies. The food filled my soul and lifted my heart in hope and determination. I would escape into Jewish wifehood.

When I told my mother that Nate and I were talking about marriage, her unhappiness and eager misery at my coming abandonment oozed from her moist eyes. "You'll never fit in with those people!" she ranted scornfully, with her feelings of superiority over my wealthy future in-laws and their Jewish accents. Listening to her, you'd think she'd been merely disguised as an orphan in order to mingle with her subjects. Nate called her The Duchess behind her back. It made me mad. It made me proud.

The next day, she was at it again. "My God, you're eighteen years old! You don't know what you're doing! You're throwing away your life!" But she couldn't stop me. Whether she was right or wrong in her dire pronouncements was irrelevant to me, immaterial, beside the point. Kenny had left; my friends were in school; my feet hurt from boring workdays of hot lights and runways; my mother was driving me crazy.

And I was finally getting into the Dick-and-Jane book. Since second grade I had coveted that smiling family on those pages; now I would be the happy wife standing in the doorway of the neat little house, my child running to meet the red-cheeked dad walking home with his newspaper and pipe, followed by Spot the dog, wagging his tail. I was going to live happily ever after. I really was.

Aunt Goldie gave an engagement party for Nate and me, friends entertained us at lunch and dinner. And my bridal shower! Tomato juice cocktails and chicken a la king and fruit salad and popovers and chocolate pecan sundaes. Handsomely wrapped and ribboned gifts piled high that I opened to a chorus of oh's and ah's. Embroidered handkerchiefs, two lace-trimmed night-gowns, a mauve chiffon scarf, a housecoat, two irons, a cookbook, lounging pajamas, a pair of leather gloves, a black slip, a set of towels monogrammed with my new initials, an ivory tablecloth. And best of all, as my beau-tiful engagement ring was dutifully admired, I saw the envy in my girlfriends' eyes—and in their mothers'—at my catch.

Seventeen

I AM COMPLAINING to Dr. Herman about the way Nate's father speaks to his mother. "He treats her like shit. It's painful to watch."

"Oh really?"

His sarcasm is unusual. It makes me angry but also hopeful. It means this could be one of the times he'll actually say something.

"And how does Nate treat her?"

"The same. Awful."

"A pretty good reason for you to marry him."

"That's ridiculous. I married him because I fell in love."

"Perhaps it felt like love."

"What do you mean felt like. It was. It was love."

"Sometimes what seems like love is something else," he says.

"Like what?"

"Like getting back at your mother."

Now I'm getting mad. "You're not listening! I told you! I fell in love and got married."

"And when you saw how badly Nate treated his own mother you knew he could protect you from her."

"I don't know what you're talking about," I mutter.

"I'm talking about your repressed fear and anger toward your mother. I'm talking about marrying a man who'd not only keep her away, but also express your anger for you."

I'm reminded of the first time I heard Nate yell at his mother that day in his darkroom. I remember the way it thrilled me, the way it made my heart swell, and it is as if Dr. Herman has sorted out and beamed a light on a tangle of feelings as familiar as my hand and as remote as the moon. I sense a lifting of my soul that feels like something sweet, like relief, like love. I want never to leave this place, this couch, that's becoming as comfortable as a cloud; this place where I feel worthy and understood and half in love with the disembodied voice behind me. I want him to love me back. He is old enough to be my father, a head shorter and bald, but the way I am being known by him in this room begins to feel very sexy. Lately I've been wondering what it would be like to be married to Jacob Herman. To live with his kindness and skill; to be accepted.

"I stood up to Nate, yesterday," I tell him, proudly. "Twice."

"Oh?" he says.

"When he came downstairs for breakfast, I was sitting at the table reading the the newspaper and he grabbed it out of my hand. As usual. But this time I grabbed it back."

"What did he do?"

"Sat down and glared at me. And that's not all," I go on. "I told him to get his guns out of the house."

"He has guns?"

"Yeah. Two loaded guns. On the shelf of his closet. With children in the house! I told him to get rid of them."

"Good for you," he says.

"No, it wasn't me, it was you. I kept wondering what you would think. I swear to God I heard your voice telling me what to say."

"You're giving me power I don't have. It was you speaking, not me. You've projected my voice because I treat you with respect as the worthy person you are. So you put the words in my mouth that you're unwilling to call your own, to take responsibility for."

"Not exactly unwilling. Afraid."

"Okay, afraid. That's fair. What are you afraid of?"

"More insults," I say. "More contempt. Afraid of feeling awful again."

"But you've demonstrated that you're not afraid. Standing up to Nate didn't come from me, it came from your new self-worth. It belongs to you now. How does it feel?"

I close my eyes. How does it feel? I'm not sure. It is too new. The air-conditioner in the window hums. Someone coughs next door in the dentist's office. Dr. Herman's four o'clock uses too much perfume. I lie there smelling it. Shalamar. I saw her once, when like a jealous sibling I came early to spy on her coming out of the office. She was a pale, skinny thing about my age with a woebegone expression and stringy hair.

Finally I say, "It feels odd. Like I've left something behind that belongs to me."

"Something you don't need."

"Yeah," I say, breathing, feeling a sweet wave of relief.

"So did he get rid of the guns?"

"No. He told me to mind my own business. I called his father to come get them."

"Did he?"

"That afternoon, while Nate was playing golf. Then last night when I was in bed he yelled '*Where are they!*' I slid down and pulled the covers over my head. He yanked them off swearing a blue streak and his face got the color of raw beets. I gave them to your father, I told him. 'You *what*?' he hollered. Your father, I said. I gave them to your father."

"Then what happened?" Dr. Herman asked.

"He stood there in a kind of trance. There was nothing he could do or say. His guns were gone. His father took his guns."

"The ultimate castration," Dr. Herman says.

"Yeah," I say.

"And the world didn't come to an end," he says. I hear him shift in his chair behind me, which means more is coming. "And speaking of your husband, I find it significant that this is the first time you've talked about him in months. We have to work through the reasons."

But I don't want to talk about Nate. I don't know why and I don't want to work through the reasons. I'm standing up to him now, aren't I? I have more self-worth now, don't I? Even Dr. Herman says so. Someone in the building is playing a piano. "Blue Moon," over and over. I lie there, listening, until he tells me that our time's up.

Eighteen

TWO WEEKS AFTER Nate and I announced our engagement, the country was at war. Nate, certain to be drafted, wondered if we should postpone our wedding. I shook my head. Stuck with my foolish fantasies, there was no way I'd let him get away, and we went ahead with our plans to marry on December 25. Christmas was an odd choice for a Jewish wedding but I didn't care—I was getting married. Nate had picked the date, initiating a 25-year pattern of dogmatic, unilateral decision-making.

One day when my mother came home from work she announced that she wanted to take the three of us out to dinner to celebrate.

I looked at her in surprise. I knew she couldn't afford it. "You don't have to do that, Mom, really."

"I'm the mother of the bride," she said. "It's the proper thing to do."

"Well, okay, if you really want to," I said, too pleased and proud to be suspicious.

"We'll go to Grubers. Invite Nate for Saturday night and make a reservation for seven-thirty."

"Grubers!" I cried. "Grubers is too expensive! Let's go to Aurora for spaghetti . . . "

"I should say not. What am I, the poor relation or something? We're going to Grubers."

Ignoring the tiny worm of apprehension I felt moving around in my midsection, I made the reservation.

Gruber's was *the* place to be on Saturday night, and sweeping into the restaurant in her good beige silk and high heels with her hair upswept like Betty Grable's, my mother looked like the sister of the bride. We were shown to our table and given menus. She recommended the vichyssoise or shrimp cocktail, and the filet mignon, as if she dined at Grubers every night. She selected a Bordeaux from the wine list, offered cocktails. She was animated, gracious, charming. I watched her proudly but warily. I didn't know how long this new mom would last. Or could she have been jerked by my imminent departure into an ongoing pattern of good behavior? Could that actually happen? I felt a tiny, secret stirring of hope.

We had Manhattans. We had shrimp cocktails. Filets mignon with mushroom sauce. Wild rice and baby carrots. We had salads. The waiter passed warm rolls. My mother toasted our happiness with her fine Bordeaux. For dessert she swept away my protests and ordered a baked Alaska in honor of the occasion. By now my pride had changed to panic. She had easily spent a month's salary. When the waiter wheeled the sparkling dessert to our table I could barely swallow.

But I had underestimated her. When the check came my dressed-up mom sat on her hands and looked around. She took out her compact and carefully applied lipstick. She put a cigarette in her mouth and leaned forward for Nate's match. The leather folder with the bill discretely tucked inside lay there and I saw what was coming. My fiance was getting stiffed. And with no money of my own—I turned my paychecks over to my mother—I sat red-faced and helplessly mortified until Nate finally opened the folder and paid. And never let me forget it.

"How could you do that!" I screamed when we got home. "How *could* you!"

"He can afford it," she said, pulling off her dress.

Staring at her as she calmly tied on her robe, I thought of that time at the deli when she lifted someone's umbrella.

"I'm going to read awhile," she said. Picking up her book she went into the living room.

I took a deep breath. In 42 days I'll be away from her forever and she'll never embarrass me like that again. She won't have the power. I'll be a free spirit. Independent. No one to tell me what to do. I'll have a beautiful house, plenty of money. A handsome husband. I'll have my darling Nate—so generous tonight after my mother's disgraceful behavior, such a gentleman.

The following Sunday, my future mother-in-law called my mother.

"Florence," she said, "we want to make the wedding. We'll make it nice, in a nice hotel. With music, dancing. A bar."

"No, Becky," my mother said. "The bride's family makes the wedding."

She called again the next morning. "My cousin's son married a poor girl and they let *her* make the wedding. A beautiful wedding. I was there."

She was lucky my mother didn't kill her. All she did was slam down the phone and tell me to have Nate call his stupid mother off.

But it was true that we couldn't afford a wedding. "I just want to go somewhere and get married,"I told her.

"No way," she said. "That Becky thinks I can't give my own daughter a proper wedding. I'll show her."

Proper. There was that word again, alarming me. "Mom, I don't want a proper wedding . . . "

But she was on her way to the telephone. I heard her call in sick. Then she slammed into the bedroom and emerged in her black coat with the fake fur collar and the black turban that set off her Katharine Hepburn bones. She left the apartment without a word. I didn't ask her where she was going. I didn't want to know. All I could do was count the days again until I'd be married and she was out of my life.

As I walked home from the bus after work that night it started to snow. Still chilled from modeling swimsuits in a resort-wear fashion show, by the time I got to our apartment I was shivering. My mother opened the door before I could get my key in the lock.

"Babbie!" she said, grinning. "We're having a wedding dinner for 40 in a private room at the Hotel Alcazar! And Aunt Sally is taking you shopping for your wedding gown! Tomorrow!"

I sat down in my coat. "You didn't," I moaned.

She opened her eyes wide. "Didn't what?"

"How could you!"

She looked innocently around the room.

"You went to them. You begged."

"The hell I did," she snapped. "I don't beg."

"What would you call it?" I said, bitterly.

"They owe you. I merely reminded them they owe you."

"That must have gone over big."

"Look, all these years of the Depression I'm alone raising two kids, they're making money. Not a helping hand from them. Not a penny or a telephone call or a dinner invitation. Isn't Marvin your rich big-shot uncle? Doesn't he have a chain of bakeries? He can pay for a lousy wedding dinner and some flowers. Big deal. Your Uncle Sid got started in business with our money. Like I said, they owe you. It's time they came across."

I rubbed my forehead—my head was splitting.

"All you do is kvetch—I'd think you'd be happy I went out and got you a proper wedding." She looked at me. "So take your coat off already."

"I'm too cold."

"Kvetching again."

"You'd be cold too if you had to wear swimsuits in 15 degree weather."

161

She headed into the kitchen. "Oh, you're just hungry again. I picked up some chop suey on the way home."

I have to admit the wedding was lovely, my gown and veil beautiful. The ceremony was held in the chapel of the Euclid Avenue Temple, Rabbi Brickner officiating. I floated stiffly down the aisle, a virgin bride on Uncle Sid's arm. He handed me over to Nate, and sat down.

Elegant in his striped trousers and cutaway, Nate gripped my arm. His face was red and he was swaying slightly; I smelled whiskey on his breath. He smiled at me, but it was the grin of a husband who turns into a hideous stranger in a dream. I felt a strange lightness in my midsection and knees. Although the Rabbi began chanting in Hebrew, all I heard was the sound of my mother weeping from her seat in the front row. These were not a parent's sentimental sniffles, they were loud wrenching sobs as if I were about to be executed. I was unnerved, embarrassed, scared. Why was she crying like that? Did she know something I didn't?

Afterwards we went to the Hotel Alcazar for the wedding dinner. I wished Kenny were there with me, but he was in Antigua running a bull-dozer. The room was fragrant with flowers and scented candles; the table had gold-edged place cards and a tall wedding cake with a bride and groom perched on top. My mother was a radiant hostess in a long mauve gown. Becky, short and round with brown hair and pretty blue eyes, was dressed in tight blue lace and diamonds. Seated at the head table with Nate and me, her husband, Morris, my mother, and the wedding party, she looked at Nate adoringly with wet eyes and called him Sonny Boy. The food was delicious—roast beef with tiny potatoes and asparagus. Wine was served; there were toasts. Uncle Sid got drunk.

Back at the apartment I changed into my going-away suit. Nate picked me up and loaded the car with my luggage as my mother watched. I hugged her goodbye and got into the car as she and Nate nodded coolly to each other in a kind of reluctant acknowledgment of their unwilling connection. As we left for our honeymoon the last thing I saw in the pale light of the garage was my mother's mournful face. Tears of guilt, of relief, ran down my cheeks. Nate handed over his handkerchief and smiled at me as if I were crying with happiness.

My escape was short-lived. Nate was drafted a few months after we were married and there I was, back with my mother again. Still moving, she decided on New York this time. Kenny was now living and working in Manhattan, and after Nate was sent overseas my mother and I settled there in an apartment on East 79th St.

Home again with my mother, job-hunting every day, eating dinner with her at neighborhood restaurants every night, my marriage felt as if I had dreamed it. Brushing my hair in the mirror, putting on lipstick, I looked as I always had: young, soft-faced, virginal, and in spite of the marriage ceremony at Euclid Avenue Temple with Rabbi Brickner officiating, in spite of the wedding gown and wedding dinner and the regular sex, my marriage seemed to have evaporated into some kind of wishful thinking or hallucination. It was as if I'd been running in place, as if my powerful mother had contrived the Second World War to keep me stuck with her forever. I got a little stab of surprise every time I noticed the wedding band on my finger.

One evening I ran into a friend from Cleveland and was late getting home.

I hadn't got my key in the door when my mother flung it open.

"Where were you!"

"I ran into Lenore Goldsmith on Lexington and we went for coffee. Remember Lenore? She's in New York, living on.. . . ."

"You're an hour late!"

"Sorry, we got to talking and I guess I forgot the time."

"You guess you forgot the time," she mimicked. "You guess you forgot the time. Babbie, you're so inconsiderate. After all I've done for you, after all my sacrifices, you keep me waiting like this."

"So you shouldn't have waited," I said. "You should have gone on ahead."

She heaved a sigh. "You know something? You're just not mature enough to be married. You're not ready for the responsibilities." She put her hands on her hips and looked at me. "If you get pregnant I suppose you'll leave the baby with me to raise," she said proudly, doing her Mother Of The Year routine. Leave my child with her? It was actually funny, but I didn't know whether to laugh or cry.

"There's a new Chinese restaurant opened up on Third and 68th," she said. "Let's go."

She put on her hat, adjusting it carefully in the mirror, and we left the apartment.

I got a job modeling Bernice Charles hats for department store buyers on the fourth floor of a building at 711 Fifth Ave. It was easier to pull hats on and off than dresses and suits, and the location was an improvement over the Seventh Avenue garment district. Lined up on stands in the back room stood a rainbow of large-brimmed picture hats that framed the face, felt cloches that covered the ears, tiny cocktail hats with glamorous veils, Empress Eugenie hats that dipped over one eye, off-the-face hats, hats that tied under the chin. I was the only full-time model, but when we were busy, Shirley, the receptionist, modeled with me. We wore plain black dresses and high heeled pumps, changed hats in the back, paraded out to the customers buying for Saks or Macy's or Gimbel's, endured hearing the salesmen's same pitch and tired jokes over and over, and smiled smiled smiled. Shirley was single and stuck in her job, but I was only marking time until my husband came home from the war and I could begin my real life as Nate's loving wife.

Nineteen

WHEN THE WAR was over, Nate's outfit was among the first to arrive in New York because it had been en route from Italy to the Pacific when the Bomb was dropped on Hiroshima and Nagasaki.

I am at the pier when his troop ship docks. It is exciting, thrilling; my husband is returning to his war bride, me, after fighting bravely for his country. It is like a movie. I am starring in my own movie. I am June Allyson, I am Myrna Loy, I am one of those perfect movie wives of the forties, a shining celluloid image with no history and a happy ending. No longer a wandering daughter of violence with my nose pressed wistfully against other people's windows, I am in the mainstream, splendid in my respectability. There is no way for me to know how seductive and dangerous these fantasies will be for me, or of my awakening to their mean and ironic afterlife.

I had to go back home to await Nate's release from the ship, so we didn't actually meet until after midnight. After our two-year separation, the six-hour wait for his call was interminable. Our few times together before he was sent overseas had been influenced by the drama and romance of war, and I had missed him terribly, or the idea of him, or the dream of myself: safe, married, content.

When he finally telephoned, I packed a bag and took a cab to his hotel. And there he was, opening the taxi door, my lost liberator returned to me, looking splendid in his officer's uniform, his buttons and captain's bars gleaming, just as I had daydreamed. We hugged. I touched his face and he kissed me. We were still in the movie.

It was a third-rate hotel off Broadway. Apologizing, Nate said he had called every hotel in town and it was the only room left in New York. I didn't mind—the sleeping desk clerk and shabby lobby and creaking elevator added to the romance. Upstairs in the corridor we heard the muffled voices of a man and woman arguing and a slamming door. Nate unlocked number 235. The room smelled of cigar smoke. There was a bed, a beat-up dresser, a chair. The window shade was torn and there were water stains on the faded wallpaper. A telephone was ringing and ringing somewhere.

We were as shy with each other as awkward strangers or teenagers. (It was, after all, a forties movie.) Nate took my bag from my fist. We smiled, we asked each other how we were, if we had eaten, if we were tired. Still, by daylight we had made love twice on the squeaking bed. I was surprised by the sex. After such a long separation I had expected something more fraught and portentous, an earthshaking, yielding, fusion. But it felt a little violent and much too quick.

We slept until noon. Then we went to Rumplemeyers and ordered a huge breakfast.

"Your blouse is too tight," Nate said.

"Too tight?" I looked down. "No it isn't."

"It's too tight. Don't wear it again."

I looked at him. He was glaring at me. "You're upset!" I said in surprise.

"You're goddamn right I'm upset. Look at you. I told you. Get rid of that thing."

Well, I thought, he's not himself. Of course, he's not himself. How could he be—just home, just off a troop ship after two years in a horrible war. I took his hand. "Okay."

The next morning we were on a train to Cleveland that was so jammed we had to sit on the floor until a group of enlisted men got off at Syracuse. Nate stowed our bags overhead and we slid into the seats. The crowded car was so eerily quiet and Hitler so recently defeated, it was like floating silently in a dream of the war's end.

Nate had spent the war in Fogio, Italy, identifying military installations from aerial photographs taken of enemy terrain. With his Captain's prestige, he had his own boy—a 12-year-old street urchin—to shine his shoes, run his errands, and with his street smarts turn up a bottle of Chianti, real meat, an egg. Although he studied air photos on the ground instead of taking them from the air, it was if he had fought through Anzio or Okinawa or the Bulge, a hero home from the war. I, too, would give him his hero's welcome and follow him gladly to the suburban good life of evenings of bridge and baby showers, refrigerators and Chryslers, wall to wall carpeting, tasseled draperies that covered picture-windows with a pull on a string, supermarkets, miraculous grainy pictures on tiny television screens and machines that washed dishes.

"Where are the war bonds I sent home?" Nate asked after a while.

"I have them," I said. "Well, some of them."

"What do you mean some of them?"

"I used six or seven—"

"You *what*?"

"Used them. Just six or seven—"

He stared at me. "You were supposed to save those bonds!"

"Nate, I did. I saved half—well, almost half, but . . ."

"But what!"

"Shh, Nate, lower your voice . . . ."

"Don't shh me! What the hell did you spend them on!"

"I didn't *spend* them on anything. I used them to live on. I had to."

"But you were working!"

"Not all the time."

"Not all the time! Why the hell not?" He narrowed his eyes and glowered at me in his captain's uniform as if he were interrogating a Nazi spy. "What were you doing?"

"Moving to New York, looking for a job—"

"So who told you to move?" He glared at me. "Yeah. Your mother. Your pathetic, disgusting mother. I'm in the armed forces, I'm in Italy serving my country and you two go ahead and have yourselves a time on my war bonds."

I turned to the window and saw his suddenly ugly face reflected in the glass. Who was this person?

"I sent those bonds to you in good faith. I trusted you," he went on bitterly.

We sat in silence. I was too furious to speak. As the train rocked along, I closed my eyes and made my plans. I'll get my bag down, take out the bonds, throw them in his face and get off at the next stop. But when the train rattled and groaned to a stop in Pittsburgh I sat there. I didn't move. My mother was waiting for me to return to her, defeated and contrite, saying I told you so.

After I missed a second period I went to the doctor. In the examination room I was handed a smock and told to strip from the waist down except for my shoes. (The shoes part puzzled me, but I followed orders and soon learned they were a necessary part of the humiliation that was to follow.) The heels of my shoes in stirrups, eyes glued to the ceiling, the doctor's head disappeared between my pushed-apart knees. I was told to relax (relax!) while feeling his rubber-gloved hand painfully probing deeply hidden organs I didn't know I had. He finally removed the hand that felt like a fist, pulled off the rubber glove and told me what I had already figured out. I was stunned anyway. Even then I knew I was finished with something. With being young.

But as time passed my body's proud blooming gave me such me a grand feeling of value and connection, it was as if being joined to my baby had linked me to the world. Going to the supermarket, to lunch with friends, to the movies, I basked in people's glances and smiles at my looming motherliness. At night in bed, in the dark, I touched my tender rounding breasts and stroked my round pink abdomen. But when it began to outdistance my breasts and undulate with my baby's restless movements, I started to worry. How was this growing invader punching my insides ever going to get out of my body? How did that happen? Yes, I knew about dilating; I read. But I didn't believe it. My stomach was getting too damn big to believe it.

It was a difficult birth. I went into labor during the day and called Nate. He was too busy to come home, he said, and sent his sister to ride with me in the ambulance. So I called my mother, who, still in motion, had moved back to Cleveland from New York. She said she would meet me at the hospital.

She arrived at my bedside minutes before Nate. Coming into the hospital room he glared at her. Adversaries from the moment they met, my mother and Nate were now engaged in all-out war. He wanted a Jewish wife who would light the *shabbas* candles, make chopped liver, and look like the *shiksas* on the society pages of the *Cleveland News*. But he saw the threat. I might become an independent fire-brand like my mother, instead of a wife who knew her place and did what she was told, like his. He tried to push my mother out of our lives but she hung on for dear life and the lines were drawn in the battle for my soul. It was a wordless fight, both using their heavy ammunition—

Nate's a silent glare or a door-slamming stalk from the room; hers a stony refusal to back off or let anything prevent her from doing what she was determined to do—namely, stay in my life, proclaim her rightful turf. I admired her awesome tenacity and thick skin in the face of Nate's contemptuous treatment. I also hated it.

Once again my escape had turned around on me and I was right back where I started. Only this time there were two of them making me miserable, each trying to pull me away from the other, like children fighting over a rag doll. Now I had a double dose of misery trying to please Nate and still be attentive to my mother's complaints and demands for attention. My half-conscious escape plan had backfired, and all I felt was a kind of helpless fury at them both. Afraid of my mother's temper and fragility and brilliance, I sneaked money to her from my grocery allowance, gave her invitations to family outings I hoped she wouldn't accept, took care of her during her asthma attacks, visited and called her regularly.

"I'll be back later," Nate said, when he saw my mother settle into the chair. As he left, a student nurse came in and stuck a thermometer in my mouth. She was about my age, already moving in that brisk, impersonal manner of her profession, her self-confidence crackling the sodden, moist air and thick smells of the hospital room. I watched her gliding in and out in her soundless, immaculately-white shoes and crisp student's uniform, reading the thermometer, taking my blood pressure, filling the water pitcher, bringing clean towels, folding the blanket neatly at the foot of the bed. Feeling a cruel wave of envy, I imagined her dates with boys, her autonomy, her Sunday dinners with proud parents, her sweet freedom—while I was nailed to this bed, pinned down by pain and a baby taking its time in my huge stubborn belly. I began to cry. Looking alarmed, the nurse fled the room.

My mother was reading, the picture of utter calm, as if I weren't in labor. The sight of her sitting there quietly with her nose in a book as I moaned with pain helped me get through each contraction. Surely she wouldn't sit reading *A Bell For Adano* if I were going to die here with my unborn baby.

She had learned such discipline in the Home. Called by the numbers which had replaced her name, she was awakened in her 100-bed dormitory by the monitors at four-thirty in the morning, and marched in enforced silence with the other children, two by two, into the lavatory where she washed in cold water and brushed her teeth with Ivory soap. If it was Wednesday she went to the basement for her weekly bath and change of clothes, where the older girls scrubbed the younger, fifty at a time, in the large pool. After getting into her uniform she was inspected; if found wanting in cleanliness she was given demerits or slapped.

Letter writing was restricted to one day a month and incoming and outgoing mail was censored by Dr. Wolfenstein, who must have seemed more remote, stern and punishing than God himself. Sometimes Anna's mother—Florence's grandmother—sent her a dime or quarter, but if it was found it was confiscated. If she complained in a letter to her grandmother about the food or work assignments or discipline, or if she begged to be taken away, the words were blacked out and she was given 50 to 100 demerits. She also got 100 demerits and slapped for going over the fence for food, for not saying yes sir, for unshined shoes, for throwing snow balls. If she got 21 or more demerits in a week she had to eat all her meals standing up for seven days, was made to stand in the prayer hall for the week and was not allowed to eat Friday night's precious *kuchen* or biscuits. But as miserable as life was, the ultimate threat and fear was expulsion, because she knew she had nowhere else to go.

As in battle she had developed the discipline of a soldier. She taught herself shorthand and bookkeeping when she was out of work and out of money; alone, she drove me to her sister's every summer over 500 miles of winding roads, some unpaved. She made her meager income provide a car, food, clothes and a roof for the three of us, support for her hated mother, college tuition for Kenny, all the while smelling of lilacs and looking like a duchess.

Now the contractions were so close together and long I was howling with pain and grabbing onto the bedposts behind me.

My mother shot out of her chair and charged into the corridor.

"Give my daughter something for the pain!" she yelled. "She's in pain!"

"The doctor didn't order any medication," the nurse said.

"For God's sake, she's been in hard labor for hours! Hours! You have to do something!"

"I'm sorry. I can't give her any medication without the doctor—"

"Shut *up*! My mother snapped. "There's the telephone. Call him." Then: "Don't you shake your head at me!"

"Dr. Lang left orders not to be disturbed."

"He *what*?"

"I'll get the resident on duty," the nurse said.

"You call Dr. Lang right now and get him here or I'll break every goddamn bone in your goddamn body." Anyone within the sound of her strangled hiss knew without a doubt that she meant every word. She was magnificent. Listening, I wept with relief. Two years later she heard that Dr. Lang had died of cancer. "I wished it on him," she told me, cheerfully.

But she always came through in a crisis. When I was ten, someone jumped on her running board as she drove home from work and grabbed her purse. It held her entire life savings. Ever since the bank failures, she had kept the money wrapped in a rubber band, tucked inside a secret compartment of her purse.

I pictured her in the car. A hot summer day. The windows are open. She has stopped at a red traffic light. Her purse is nearby for comfort on the passenger seat, her hoarded, rolled-up fives and tens held snugly within. And her glasses. Her Flame Red lipstick and Sand face powder. Her comb and keys. Her handkerchief with the pink rose embroidered in the corner. The thief suddenly appears on the running board, reaches into the open window and grabs her purse; a microsecond too late she lunges for it but he is too fast and she stares helplessly at his back as he runs like the wind down an alley, her purse dangling from his fist. Now the car behind her is honking; the light has turned green. She pulls the car over to the side of the road, leans her forehead against the steering wheel and sobs.

She came home that day, hung up her good suit and called up an old boyfriend. The next day she had a month's rent and food money. The day after that she declared bankruptcy. Then and only then, she fell apart.

She went in the bedroom and started to bawl. The sound was like a wail. It made me feel like crying. I put my hands over my ears. Her fear filled the apartment like rot, drifting airborne to the rooms. I could smell it. I smelled her fear. I went outside and sat on the stoop for a long time. After a while I wiped my eyes and nose on my shirt bottom and went to the library.

The nurse must have taken my mother's remorseless threat to her person seriously, because in short order an intern appeared in my hospital room, and soon afterward, Dr. Lang himself, who had me wheeled into the delivery room. A mask was put over my face, I was told to breathe deeply and count backward from 100. And the next thing I knew I was holding my son, Lewis, in my arms.

Andrew was born two-and-a-half years after Lewis, and Kay six years later. With each birth I felt queer stirrings of a love so pristine and powerful I thought my heart would burst. My restless and undefined confusion, my unrecognized unhappiness were reconfigured magically into that strange and profound and consuming thing: a mother; *their* mother. I drank them in, their sturdy fragility, their beauty, their neediness, their promise. I wanted to be the mother to them I didn't have. A mother like those I coveted as a child who stayed home and enforced curfews and homework. Went to PTA meetings and teacher conferences. Saved up for educations and read bedtime stories and locked up at night. Watched out for frayed wires and skates in the hall. Bandaged scraped knees. Made cookies and dentist appointments and Halloween costumes.

Having children helped me see that the idea I had of my father was all wrong; that the love I believed he had for me was pure fantasy. I don't know when he turned from a construction of my imagination to something real, from longing to anger, from fantasy to truth. It was gradual, more or less unconscious, seeping into my blood slowly over the years like a transfusion of reality—an inoculation against self-delusion. My father wasn't up there with a gun looking out for me; I now saw him standing full blown and dangerous amid the ruin he left behind.

Caught between the values of his Jewish law-abiding, hard-working parents and siblings, and his appetite for vice, he was successful at neither; beneath the charm a kind of rotting had already begun. Damaging two entire families in the havoc of his short destructive life, he was merely a roughneck with a violent trigger temper and a monumental indifference to the lives entrusted to him—his own included.

Letting go of the fantasy of my father as mythical loving protector made me feel as if I had lost part of myself. But I felt relieved, too. I thought I had finally laid him to rest. I thought it was as if he was killed twice, the second time for good. I was wrong.

Twenty

BACK IN CLEVELAND, life was hopeful, at first. My mother had returned to New York and Nate was preoccupied with the booming automobile business.

When war was declared, automobile factories had been converted into the manufacture of military vehicles, and car dealers found themselves out of business overnight. But Morris, my savvy father-in-law, got a government contract for the production of airplane parts, and while Nate was overseas, went into the manufacturing business. Then, when Nate came home after the war, Morris handed him the key to his Chrysler agency. It was like giving him a license to print money. Auto makers began turning out Fords, Chevrolets and Chryslers to a car-starved country as fast as they could and wherever we went—to a restaurant, the theater, the Club—people actually pushed money at Nate, begging, pleading, to be put at the top of the waiting list. He sold cars as fast as he could get them, naming his own price. The money rolled in, and thanks to his father, Nate became rich.

Morris had reached the promised land from Latvia and bestowed on his adored American-born son all that had been denied him from the pogroms, from immigration, from the Great Depression, from anti-semitism. And Nate went to college with a convertible, a pocket full of money, and his father's American Dream. Arrogant with his substantial achievements, Morris had shed his humble, immigrant values and encouraged his son to think he could buy anything he wanted to buy, and do whatever he wanted to do, and like a minor pharaoh, Nate made every decision in our marriage from where we would live to where we would go for dinner. He chose our house and our dog; he selected my clothes and our friends, our furniture and wallpaper, the paintings, the plants in the garden and the food in the refrigerator.

We embarked on the post-war good life. We traveled, sometimes to Bimini or Palm Beach or the Bahamas on our 55-foot yacht that Nate had named after me, sometimes on a plane to Europe. We were a couple within a network of other couples just like us, going to country club dances and each others' dinner parties. The men played golf and made money and the women decorated their houses and themselves from the pages of *House Beautiful* and *Harpers Bazaar*. Water from sprinkler systems sparkled on lush green lawns as gardeners attended rhododendrons, azaleas and pachysandra. Maids walked from the 8 a.m. bus on the shaded, curving streets as the ladies of the houses dressed for their 9 o'clock tennis games; afterwards, still in tennis whites, they'd go to Heinens Supermarket to shop for a dinner party, or maybe a family backyard barbecue. You noticed them in their tiny white skirts and slim brown legs among the heavier blue-collar wives. Or, if it was winter, they'd slip into soft wool dresses in jewel colors for meetings at the Hadassah, or the Ladies' Auxiliary of Mt. Sinai Hospital.

We got our hair and nails done once a week, got dressed up and danced the cha cha cha and jitterbug to big bands, drank martinis and flirted with each other's husbands. Tanned and slender, groomed and brushed, we gave huge black-tie parties at the country club and under flower-decorated tents in our backyards. We wore sweater sets of soft cashmere and pearls under mink coats in winter, and squeezed ourselves into waist-clinchers under full-skirted dresses of sheer cotton and silk in summer. Meanwhile, the McCarthy hearings, the Rosenberg executions, Governor Orval Faubus' school closings, the Birmingham civil rights riots, the Bay of

Pigs and the Berlin Wall played out their dramas like distant static, and except for locking horns with our children over sex and drugs and anti-war demonstrations (they weren't like us), it was as if we were stuck in some anthropologist's remote village, isolated and secluded, living the fifties dream on into the sixties and beyond.

One of my coats, a maroon wool, reminded me of the one my mother had somehow got Uncle Marvin to buy for me when I was twelve. All I knew at the time was that Aunt Linda called one evening to say that the coat had been delivered to her house. My mother said we would pick it up the next evening.

My mother handed me the phone. "Aunt Linda wants to talk to you."

"Babbie, when you come over to get the coat will you stay and babysit my niece for a couple of hours?" she asked.

"Aunt Linda, I can't," I said. "I have girl scouts on Tuesday night."

The next evening we rang Aunt Linda's doorbell.

"Well!" she said, opening the door. "Look who's here."

"Hello, Linda. We came for the coat," my mother said, steering me into the living room.

"I know why you came," she said, glaring at me. "It's okay for me to buy you a coat but when I ask you to do something for me, you're too busy." She took the coat out of the box. "Here," she said, throwing it at me.

Reaching, my mother caught it like a Yankee right fielder.

I went into the bathroom. I didn't want Aunt Linda to see me cry.

My mother followed me with the coat over her arm. "I don't want it! Don't make me take it! Please! Please don't make me take it!"

"Hush up," she said, tearing off some toilet paper and drying my face. "You need a winter coat." She yanked me into the living room, thanked Aunt Linda sweetly, and marched me out the door.

Eleven years later, when she observed my downstairs front closet stuffed with coats and furs, her covetous sighs made it clear she expected me to return the favor. And I did. I handed over some coats and dresses as if I was feeding an angry goddess to keep from being consumed in the fire of her envy. Once I gave her a brooch that Nate had given me, another time a garnet necklace. She wore them in front of him, as if to say, See! I won that round.

"Jesus Christ!" Nate yelled. "You gave my jewelry to that woman!"

I didn't blame him for being angry. But I didn't blame her, either. The have/have-not gap that now existed between us was too huge for her to bear. I had left her and gone on to "achieve" everything she had always wanted.

She saw me as a success because of the 55-foot *Babette* docked in Ft. Lauderdale and the big house, dismissing the despised son-in-law as irrelevant, beside the point. Once, when I hinted darkly at divorce she told me that no situation was perfect, that I had three children and I had better stay where I was. "Look at me and count your blessings," she said. "I was smart and see where it got me. Smart doesn't put food on the table like a pretty face and a rich husband." For all her brilliance she hadn't a clue as to the needs of the human soul— especially her own.

But nothing in my life was working. Weighing myself against the golf-playing country club young matrons, I failed. No matter how many golf and tennis lessons I took, or how many martinis I drank or husbands I flirted with, I felt outside it all, still the unparented kid with her nose pressed against the window. My hands broke out in hives when I played golf, the martinis made me throw up, and I even failed at adultery.

"Hello." A lowered voice on the phone. "Can you talk?"

"What?"

"It's me! George!"

"George?" I repeated stupidly.

"Remember? At the Club? You said I could call you . . . ."

I sat down with the phone. George. A hazy presence from Saturday night's alcohol dream of escape from something I couldn't even name.

"How's one o'clock?" he was saying.

It was coming back. Slow dancing to a Latin beat . . . arms holding me close . . . hips moving in sensuous rhythm . . . whisperings in my ear . . .Can I call you?

"Chagrin Falls," he went on. "Meet me at the Falls and we'll drive to a place I know for lunch . . . ."

"Oh, no, I couldn't possibly."

"But you said . . . ."

"I know," I said, face flaming. "But, see, my baby isn't feeling well . . . ."

"Okay, how about next Monday."

"Look, George, you're married, I'm married . . ."

"That didn't seem to bother you Saturday night."

"Don't call me again," I said, slamming down the phone.

Another time I actually got as far as a hotel room with a handsome blue-eyed man we had met in Phoenix at an automobile association meeting. I must have given him my phone number during our animated somewhat drunken conversation, because when he came to Cleveland from California on business two weeks later, he called me. "I haven't been able to get you out of my mind," he crooned into the telephone. "I'm at the Cleveland. Room 762. Come down. Please. Please come down. I have to see you again."

And I did. I went to room 762 and knocked softly on the door. It flew open and I looked at the blue-eyed stranger in a suit and tie standing there, smiling. I saw the double bed, the dresser, the night stand, the Bible, the easy chair, the lamp. I saw the bottle on the dresser, bourbon, I think, the ice bucket and glasses. And I left. I really did. In shame and confusion I turned on my heel and left the room.

It wasn't sex that I wanted. It was rescue. I didn't know I'd have to rescue myself.

Full of self-contempt for being a tease, I volunteered for good works, played games (golf, cards, one-upsmanship), smiling, trying, submerging myself in the suburban good life, doing subtle hidden violence to myself because it was too hard to be different.

My misery amidst such privilege made me feel guilty, which made me more miserable, further exacerbating my guilt. What was wrong with me? I couldn't understand how I could be so lucky and so unhappy. I had three great kids whom I adored, a beautiful home, jewels, closets full of designer clothes that Nate bought me. I had two maids and a loyal housekeeper, friends and travel and health and a rich husband who said he loved me. And sailing to the Bahamas from Ft. Lauderdale, I sat on the vast deck of the *Babette*, weeping.

One day before we left for one of our trips an acquaintance of Nate's began docking his yacht next to ours.

"Hey Nate!" he called. "You got a broad in a bikini cryin' up on your deck!"

"Goddamn it, watch out for my paint!" Nate yelled. "You're coming in too close! Get your bumpers down!"

I had discovered drinking. I liked the harsh near-happiness, the unjudging warmth going down like a kind friend, the way it almost obliterated what was confusing and sad in my life, everything that had gone wrong. Gin and tonics on the yacht, martinis at Grubers Restaurant, scotches at Club dances, Manhattans at dinner parties. A highball to calm my frustration as, dressed and pacing, I waited for Nate, who was always late while friends waited in their car, or the food withered and cooled at the dinner party, or the first act had already begun.

So having learned first hand of the soothing properties of gin and vermouth, I decided to offer Nate a chilled martini and a quiet half hour before dinner with the children. I reasoned it would get him in a better mood, maybe keep him from scolding and glowering at the dinner table; the meal would lose its tension and be pleasant.

"What's this?" he said.

"A martini," I said, smiling, shaking the silver art deco cocktail shaker. I had changed from jeans into a black silk dress, hose, earrings.

"A martini? What for?"

"To drink!" I said, pouring.

"I don't want any. Let's eat," he said, heading to the table. "Get the kids."

It wasn't that he didn't drink, I realized. It was that he only drank to get drunk. After which he liked to smash whatever glasses he could get his hands on. But despite occasional binges he was not a drinking man, which made his inexplicable moods all the more puzzling. One day he'd scream at me about something I bought for the house or the children or myself; a week or a month later he'd come home with a pearl bracelet or a beautiful dress. Once, after I threatened divorce, he gave me a diamond and emerald ring. I never knew if he'd glare at me when he came home and make me wonder what I had done, or be full of plans for a trip to Europe or dinner out or a barbecue for friends. He complained that I wasn't picking his roses so I took a flower arranging course, after which he yelled at me for picking too many. Then, in the midst of his hollering, the phone would ring and he'd speak with charm and wit to whomever it was, his recent rantings resonating like a strong smell in the air.

Twenty-One

"ARE YOU MARRIED?" I ask Dr. Herman.

No answer. Again.

"Well, do you have any children?"

Silence.

"Am I boring you?"

More silence.

"Jack and Charlie run into each other on the street," I say. "Hi, Jack, Charlie says, what are you doing these days? I'm a psychiatrist, Jack answers. My God, Charlie says, how can you stand to listen to people's problems like that hour after hour, day after day! Who listens? Jack says."

"Do you think I don't listen?"

"How the hell do I know? You don't talk, I can't see you, for all I know you could be reading a book. You could be sound asleep. Do you snore? It would help if you snored."

"You sound angry today," he says.

"This man isn't feeling well," I say, "and his wife takes him to the doctor. After examining him the doctor takes the wife aside. Your husband is a very sick man, but if you give him a lot of tender loving care, good nutrition and plenty of sex, he'll be okay. When they get in the car the husband asks his wife what the doctor said. You're going to die, she says."

"Is the husband in the joke Nate?" Dr. Herman asks.

"Well, I'd make a marvelous widow, wouldn't I? I'd be rich and young and beautiful and everyone would feel sorry for me."

"Is that what you want?"

"This woman goes to the doctor for a physical," I say. "When she comes home she tells her husband that the doctor said she had very nice breasts for her age. Oh yeah? the husband says. What did he say about your big fat ass? Your name didn't come up, dear, she says."

"It would be better if you talked about your anger at Nate directly in here," Dr. Herman says. "Without the jokes."

We are both silent. After a while it feels like a game to see who will blink first. But I am outmatched. I can't stand it. So I tell him the plot of a play I had just seen. I talk about the freezing weather and our travel plans to Florida for Christmas with the children. I describe my mother's new job at Thistledown Race Track and Kenny's election to president of the school board.

He sits behind me like a stone.

"Maybe I should leave now," I say.

"Our time's not up but you can leave if you wish."

"Don't you care if I stay or go?"

"What do you think?"

"Damn you, I'm out of here."

It was a bad session.

The next morning I look up Dr. Jacob Herman's address in the telephone book. I drive to his house and park across the street. Sitting in my car, staring at an ordinary house on an ordinary tree-shaded street reminds me of the way I drove to the murder house years ago and sat gazing at it. I have the same curiosity, the same need to know, the same impulse to go across the street and peek in the windows. It's a spring morning just like that one; from the car I see the bare trees beginning to green and feel the warming sun on my arm through the window. I sit there, staring, feeling ridiculous. Finally I see a woman come out and empty trash in the garbage can. She is gray haired, heavy set, and middle aged, and I am ferociously jealous of her.

Twenty-Two

BECAUSE OF MY shame at being a high school dropout, Dr. Herman suggested I enroll in college courses. His encouragement helped me drum up the nerve to take the required high school equivalency test and college entrance exam, and to my surprise I passed. And to my further surprise I actually hauled myself to Western Reserve University and with Dr. Herman's encouragement, registered for 15 hours.

Surrounded by 18-year-olds in my Western Civilization class, I felt ridiculous, over my head, once more out of sync with my surroundings. They were fresh out of high school, while I hadn't been in a classroom for years, and not very often at that. When the professor began his lecture I stared at his moving mouth and gesturing hands, heard his words, his phrases and references, noted the timbre and the rise and fall of his voice, and had no idea what he was talking about. How did I have the nerve to be in a college classroom? A high school dropout? Nate's right. I'm too stupid to do this. Sitting there in confusion and horror, I would have run out of the room but feeling the blood leave my head I was seriously afraid I'd faint.

But after the first weeks the professor stopped scaring me. I started to hear him. My paralysis left and I scribbled notes. Gradually, I was getting it. I was learning. I knew it. It was exciting, thrilling. My mind was working and I started to study like a medical student. I discovered that I didn't have to find some yellow brick road in search of a brain; it had been there in my head all along.

When my grades came I stared at the A's and they told me the world had changed. Even the bitter wind sweeping off Lake Erie into the campus parking lot had turned friendly, telling me I wasn't stuck in dumbness, I wasn't helpless, I could change my life. I didn't know how in those first exhilarating moments, but the semester of A's in my fist told me I'd figure it out. I signed up for fifteen hours again for the second semester.

I took my grades home with the pride of a fourth grader, feeling different in my skin and unimagined possibilities in my soul. Not the least of which was that Nate couldn't call me stupid any more.

"I got my grades," I said, when he came home.

"Let's see."

I handed him the card, surprised at my pounding heart.

"Well, aren't you the smart one."

I was silent.

"Well, aren't you?"

"I don't know."

"You don't know? Well, lookie here at these grades. Look at these A's. I guess I got me a smart wife."

We were in the kitchen. I turned away and went upstairs, feeling the same as when he called me stupid. Somehow, it was the same.

That night, at the Gordons' dinner party, he amazed me by announcing to everyone that I got all A's, while I slid down in my chair and emptied my wine glass. My embarrassment surprised me. Wasn't that what I wanted? To make Nate proud of me? And although he kept on bragging to anyone who would listen, to my disappointment he didn't treat me any differently at home. It was as if he had somehow made my grades his, and then dismissed me.

From the first day, I loved my Creative Writing class; here I had more to say than the 18-year-olds. One night after the children were in bed I wrote an essay for class about how my newly discovered pleasure in writing brought fresh and surprising insights to other parts of my life, from a PTA meeting to being stuck with a bore at a dinner party to listening to music. The professor liked the essay and encouraged me to submit it for publication. When the *Saturday Review* accepted it, and I actually saw "Confessions Of An Unpublished Writer," on its glossy pages, I was hooked. I knew what I wanted to do.

Soon afterward, I was recommended through the friend of a friend to a bookie who wanted to find a ghost writer for his autobiography. He called me, we discussed the project, agreed on my compensation, and arranged to meet the following Thursday for lunch at The Theatrical Grill.

I was excited about my first book assignment. Besides, the guy sounded engaging, with a interesting past. I looked forward to Thursday's meeting and to getting started.

"You're not going," Nate said, when I told him.

I was surprised. I expected him to be as pleased as I was. Wasn't he still bragging to people about my grades at Western Reserve? Hadn't he hung on his office wall a framed copy of the check the *Saturday Review* sent me? Alongside the letter of acceptance from Norman Cousins?

"Of course I'm going," I said.

"You think I'd let you to be seen with Nick Villarosa? *My* wife with Nick Villarosa? At The Theatrical Grill? No way."

"Okay, we won't go to the Theatrical, we'll go somewhere else."

"You're not going anywhere with him and you're not going to do this book. I know him. He's an ex-bootlegger two-bit bookie living on his glory days."

I felt my heart behave strangely. "I can't be seen with an ex-bootlegger? Is that what you said?"

"That's what I said."

"Let me remind you that your children's grandfather is an ex-bootlegger."

"I happen to be well aware of that," he said, dryly.

"So I couldn't be seen with my own father."

"That's right."

"He'd have to sneak into our house in the dead of night to see me and his grandchildren. Is that what you're telling me?"

"That's right, because I wouldn't let him in."

"You *what*?"

"You heard me. I wouldn't let that crook in my house."

It was as if I had been dealt a blow. It took my breath away. My father was dead and in no danger of being seen in or out of our house with me or anyone else, and the extent of my feelings of worthlessness at such gratuitous cruelty from my husband astonished and stunned me. All I could do was stare at him. I didn't realize it at the time but that was the moment my marriage ended.

Even so, I retreated. It wasn't worth the fight, the insults; it wasn't worth my despair. I backed down from a long held habit of accepting Nate's oppression. I was a wimp. But although I called Nick Villarosa and told him I'd be unable to work with him, my anger at Nate wouldn't stay buried—I felt it in my throat, in my skull, in my mouth.

I didn't tell Dr. Herman. I didn't want to talk about losing out on the book. Or my rage. As a matter of fact I had been feeling an increasing urgency to leave the analysis. Even when I fantasized about marrying Jacob Herman, I knew it would never happen. Patients were always falling in love with their analysts. It's called transference.

Something odd was happening. I couldn't seem to keep my time in Dr. Herman's office and my life with Nate balanced the way I had. Traveling the 20 blocks between the two places was making me uneasy. I saw, as if from the corner of my eye, that if I continued this therapy my marriage, my home, my family, could not survive.

Slowly, quietly, the woman I was, and the woman I was becoming, got locked into mortal conflict. It was exhausting me. It was making me nervous. Something had to go. I felt myself slipping dangerously out of my old skin and I was afraid if I didn't quit the couch, I wouldn't be able to get back in.

Twenty-Three

"IT'S TIME FOR me to move on," I announce to Dr. Herman.

"*What*?" he actually sounds surprised. This pleases me. After all this time I finally get a rise out of him.

"It's time," I say. But I sound braver than I feel. I'm not at all sure about being on my own without this safe island to return to every day. He has been father, mother, friend, doctor, educator, the perfect lover of my fantasies, liberator of my soul and voice of my unconscious mind for more than three years. He has helped me find my brain. He has helped me find work I love. It is enough. It is more than enough. It is more than I ever hoped for.

"I have to tell you that it's premature for you to leave." he clears his throat. "There's an unresolved issue."

"What unresolved issue?" I ask.

Silence.

But I know. "Well, being married to Nate is no picnic," I say. "But as my mother says, I should count my blessings."

He sits there, mute.

"Look," I go on, "there are no perfect situations. Lots of marriages have problems. Most, I bet. You know that. You of all people know that. As a matter of fact, I'm lucky. I have my children. Security and luxury. Friends. Health."

"This is beginning to sound familiar," he says.

"Familiar? What do you mean familiar?"

"Three and a half years ago you told me how lucky you were."

"But this is different. Thanks to you, this is different. I'm in school. I'm writing a novel. I'm standing up to Nate. Even you said so. I'm okay now."

"My, what a lot of protesting."

"There's nothing wrong with protesting when someone happens to be wrong. Even you can be wrong, you know."

He clears his throat. "Babette—as I said—as I have to tell you—we have more work to do here."

This time I'm the one who falls silent. My hour isn't up yet, but I push myself off the couch to my feet. Dr. Herman rises from his chair as he has done every day for three and a half years. But this will be the last time, I realize, with a stab of regret. I hold out my hand stiffly and make my fingers grip his with more resolve than I feel. I long to crawl back to the couch, to my sanctuary, to my place. I don't want to give up my hour in Dr. Herman's life to some stranger who I'm already beginning to hate.

But there is no turning back. I simply cannot face the truth of my marriage. We shake hands and I turn my head so he won't see my wet eyes.

"I'll be here when you need me," he says.

I lift my head and saunter out the door.

Twenty-Four

MY MOTHER WAS living in Florida now, working for an importer in a small office in Miami Beach. She wrote frequently, asking for money, complaining about the high cost of living, complaining about the monotony, complaining about the heat. And about Mr. Ginsberg. He was a retired toy manufacturer who had been taking her to dinner at Wolfie's, after which she'd slaughter him at Scrabble and berate him for what she called his fascist politics.

One Sunday morning she called and said Mr. Ginsberg had proposed marriage, which turned him into something of a hero to me. She even sounded pleased, sending hope into my heart. Kenny and I wanted her to accept. Desperately. Even as adults we wanted her to be Mrs. Ginsberg. Kenny was a husband, father, vice president of a paper company and president of the school board. I was married with three children, and we still longed for a mother like everyone else had, taken care of, married in her later years to a nice Jewish man, socializing with other retired couples, living in a Florida condo, inviting her grandchildren to visit during spring break, and maybe—who knows—maybe even venturing into the kitchen now and then. And in the bargain, not incidentally, letting Kenny and me alone and giving us some peace of mind. What was so bad?

But she turned Mr. Ginsberg down and restless as ever, came back to Cleveland.

"Oh Mom," I said, disappointed. "He sounded like a good guy."

We were sitting in front of the fireplace in the family room drinking coffee. Nate had had the room built after we moved in, designing himself its wet bar, huge stone fireplace with raised hearth, paneling, and the glass wall that looked out at the terrace and garden. I was never consulted. It was a comfortable room in spite of its size, especially with its abundant plants and the roses on the coffee table I had picked from the garden that morning. The children were in school and Nate at work—whatever that was. He never mentioned his auto agency or told me anything about what he actually did there; for all I knew he could have been cutting out paper dolls all day, or dealing dope. I didn't even know how much money he made. He refused to answer my questions or show me our joint income-tax returns, actually signing my name to the forms every year.

"You know Plato's idea that lovers were once one person?" my mother said, stirring sugar in her cup. "That's a bunch of hogwash. Men. They're all the same. Stanley Ginsberg just wanted a housekeeper he could sleep with." He never opened a book, she complained, his politics were disgusting, and she was sick of hearing about his son the investment banker, the blond *shiksa* wife, their brilliant children, the beautiful house in Westchester County. Besides, it was too hot in Florida in the summer. "See," she said, patting her wet upper lip, and brow. "I'm still perspiring."

I looked at her. Her face was red. "Do you feel okay?"

"Yeah. Just that I'm hot all the time."

I went to the phone and called my doctor. After asking me about her symptoms, he had his secretary make an appointment for her with Dr. Austin Weisberg, a blood specialist.

Dr. Weisberg told her she had *polycythemia rubra vera*, a blood disorder that makes too many red corpuscles. The treatment, bloodletting, seemed medieval to me, but back then it was the only known remedy. He told her to go to the Red Cross and donate a unit of blood every couple of months. Besides helping her condition, he said, she would be providing rich blood to others who need it.

After giving blood she felt better almost immediately, and soon got a job as an assistant to a businesswoman, taking care of her personal finances and correspondence, running errands, and sometimes babysitting her six-year-old son.

One day, about six months later, as I sat studying for a Sociology exam, I got a call from a manager at the May Co. He told me that while waiting to return a dress for her employer, my mother had fainted. They put her in a wheelchair, he said, and took her to the dispensary on the tenth floor, where she was resting.

"I'll be right down," I said.

She was lying on a cot with her eyes closed. It was a small windowless room with a sink and a white enamel cabinet. Typewriters clattered in the offices next door. A nurse sat in the chair reading *LIFE* magazine. She smelled of a heavy, flowery perfume and something else. Garlic.

"Mom?"

She opened her eyes. "Oh Babbie," she said. "I hope you don't mind, I told them to call you."

"What happened?

"Thanks for coming down. It was so nice of you to come down. Where's the nurse? There was a nurse in here. I must have fallen asleep."

"I'm here," the nurse said, without looking up from her magazine. She looked to be sixty-five or seventy years old and must have weighed over 200 pounds.

"My daughter's very busy," she said to the nurse. "She goes to college, she gets A's, she has three wonderful children and a big beautiful house, but when I need her, she comes, here she is. And you were so kind, too," she went on. "Thank you very much for taking care of me."

All this sweetness and light coming out of her worried me. This was not my mother.

"Oh, I didn't do nothin'," the nurse said, without looking up.

In her better days my mother would have made hash of this rank-smelling, 200-pound, chair-sitting nurse. Now, pale and sort of shrunken, she had turned into this sweet little old lady I hardly recognized.

She got to her feet and stood unsteadily, holding onto the bedpost.

I took her arm.

"Nurse," she said, with that same phony smile on her face, "don't I have a wonderful daughter?"

The nurse grunted something into her magazine.

"Come on, Ma. I'm taking you home."

"Thank you, dear."

By the time we arrived at her building, her color was better. I rode up in the elevator with her. Inside her apartment, she telephoned Dr. Weisberg and told him what had happened.

"He wants me to come in for a blood test tomorrow at three," she said when she hung up.

"I'll pick you up at 2:30," I said, heading for the door.

"Do you have to go? So soon? How about a cup of tea?" She was staring at me greedily as if, like my dresses and coats, I could give her my youth and health.

I shook my head and got out of there while I still had the clothes on my back.

Dr. Weisberg called me the following Tuesday. "I got the lab report," he said.

Feeling a small stab of fear, I wondered why he was calling me instead of my mother.

"It doesn't look good," he went on.

"She's giving too much blood, right?"

"No, I'm afraid it's more—worse—than that."

I waited.

"Leukemia," he said. "Acute. She's got acute leukemia."

I felt like I was falling. "But there must be some mistake! How could she have leukemia! Her blood's too rich for leukemia!"

"Not any more. Now it's the opposite. Now it's her white corpuscles that are on the rampage. It happens sometimes. Polycythemia sometimes turns into leukemia. We can keep her alive for a while with blood transfusions, but I have to tell you it doesn't look good."

I was staggered. She drove me crazy but I didn't want her to leave me. Not like this. Not bleeding to death. I had wanted her away, far away, maybe on a cruise somewhere warm with a captive audience of passengers she could instruct on politics and literature, dressed to the nines, still her formidable self. Or married. Okay, not to Mr. Ginsberg, married to a professor at the University of Florida, maybe holding Saturday afternoon salons for the faculty and the brightest students.

"Don't tell her," I whispered into the phone, as if she were still the omnipotent mother of my childhood who heard everything.

"She'll never find out from me," he said. "She couldn't handle it."

"So what will you tell her?" I was still whispering.

"That she's anemic and needs blood."

I imagine his call to her. She isn't on a cruise in the Bahamas or holding court at the University of Florida, she is alone in her small apartment, wondering for the thousandth time why she keeps fainting. As she waits for Dr. Weisberg's call with the answer, she feels a sharp stab of fear. She makes a cup of tea. Feeling weak, she lies down on the couch. The tea grows cold. At last, the telephone rings. She hurries to the kitchen, picks up the telephone and listens to Dr. Weisberg's glib reassurances. I wonder if she believes him.

After being tossed around like history's toy by the era of immigration and Prohibition's violence and the Great Depression, after not being broken by any of it— not by losing her immigrant father before she was three years old, not by her heartless mother, or the poverty, or the Dickensian orphanage; not by the murders or widowhood or single motherhood, wasn't leukemia too much? How can so much rotten luck be dumped onto one insignificant person?

The library was in a small suburban building in the neighborhood, not at all like the grand marble palace I entered the other times I researched a parent's death. As I put on my coat I was twelve years old again, glancing over my shoulder, afraid my mother would catch me looking up her secrets, afraid of what I would find.

"I need a book on disease, please." I said to the librarian.

She looked up from her desk. "What kind of disease?" I smelled the hamburger and onions she had for lunch.

"Blood," I said, absurdly nervous. She walked over to a shelf and withdrew a volume called *Symptoms*. "Start with this."

I took off my coat and sat down at one of the tables. Someone was coughing. A man and woman at the next table had their heads together, whispering. A student pushing a book cart rumbled by.

I opened the book and looked up "Leukemia" in the index.

Leukemias are a group of diseases with uncontrolled production of ineffectual white blood cells . . . . red blood cells and platelets, are crowded out . . . . Half of all the patients with the acute form survive between three and four months . . . .

It was like reading her death sentence.

I thought I had finally put some emotional distance between myself and my mother. But my analysis with Dr. Herman had stirred up all the pushed-down anger I hadn't let myself feel. Her presence that I had longed for as a child became terrifying and infuriating, the face I had thought beautiful contorted into a witch's features, her melodious voice became a cackle, her shapely hands, claws. I couldn't bear the sight of her and when she was with me I counted the hours, minutes, seconds, until she would leave my house. And now, here I was, dripping tears all over a library book announcing her death.

Three months. Fifty percent survived only three months. But first her liver, spleen and lymph nodes would become enlarged and sore. There would be weight loss and infections. Fatigue and malaise. Bruising and general bleeding. Followed, sooner instead of later, by death. I kept on reading and wiping my eyes until the librarian came over and asked me if I was all right. I blew my nose and nodded. I was used to reading up on death in the library.

As my mother and I went for her blood transfusions, as her plasma thinned and sickened and then got pumped up with fresh fluid, I was discovering how complicated, how bottomless, our own blood relationship was, and how deep and rich her thinning blood felt as it bonded to mine. I saw that she was neither the worshiped icon of my childhood nor the long-delayed object of my anger. We were simply mother and daughter, woven together by blood and history.

Rejuvenated after each transfusion she went back to work until I got the dreaded, expected telephone call. Then I would take her the food she was too weak to get herself and almost too weak to eat, and we would make our routine trip to the hospital for more blood. After each transfusion she fought her way back to an increasingly poor recovery, struggling to a more and more diminished strength. I watched helplessly as the life-giving blood circulating in her veins betrayed her—the same blood that had fed me in her womb, nurtured her remarkable brain and her ill-starred life; the juice that gave her the strength to get the three of us through the murders and those tough years.

Kenny was now living in a New York suburb, doing well in business, married and the father of two sons. I was raising three children, working hard in college, trying to change my life. She—we—hadn't done so bad. My old yearnings for another kind of mother who didn't give me confusing feelings of shame and pride and love and hate were evaporating like vapor into admiration for her life and for her ongoing, monumental fight. I saw what it cost her. She was still teaching me about courage.

At first Nate had little to say about my trips back and forth to her apartment and the hospital. Maybe it was just his relief that she wasn't coming to the house as often. Or remorse because of his treatment of her. Or could it be that she reminded him of the inevitability of death, including even his own? One time, to my astonishment, I found him leaving her hospital room. He had brought her a milkshake. Guilt, I thought, combined with the specter of death was a great leveler to the arrogant.

Twenty-Five

NATE AND I were just about to have a late dinner one evening when the phone rang. He hadn't come home until 9 o'clock because the auto agency stayed open on Thursday nights. The children were in bed.

"It's my mother," I said, coming back to the table. "I need to get over there."

"Sit down and eat."

"She needs another blood transfusion," I said, putting on my coat.

"You're not listening. I told you to sit down. You're going to stop being at that woman's beck and call. I'm goddamn sick of it and it's going to stop," he said, staring at me through his glasses.

I turned away from his withering look. "I have to get her to the hospital."

"Sit down. Your food's getting cold. She can take a cab."

"She can't take a cab, Nate, she's sick and alone and needs someone with her."

"Why does it always have to be you?"

"Because I'm all she has." I cut a slice of the meatloaf that was on the table, took one of the baked potatoes from the platter and grabbed some bread.

"That's her own fault. It's her own fault she doesn't have any friends. I'm sick of that woman interfering in my life. The witch calls and you run. I'm sick of it. In case you've forgotten, you have a husband and three children." He took off his glasses and polished them carefully with his napkin. "Look," he said, glancing up, "I've been patient. For months. Very patient. Didn't I visit her and bring a milkshake?"

Well, yes, I thought, a milkshake. Wonderful. And a visit. Terrific. I looked at him sitting at the head of the table leaning back in his chair with his arms folded like some potentate or godfather. I wanted to push the meat-loaf in his face. I went into the kitchen.

He got up and followed me. "I said you're not going."

"Nate, she's got to eat," I said, wrapping the meat loaf and potatoes in waxed paper.

"If she'd lower herself to set foot in her own kitchen she could get her own goddamn dinner."

"I told you. She needs another blood transfusion."

"So they have food in the hospital. Tell her to take a cab," he said, again.

"No," I said, spooning jello into a jar.

He picked up the phone. "Then I will."

I took it out of his hand. He grabbed it back. I stopped the dial tone. "Nate, she's dying!" I whispered.

"The sooner the better," he muttered.

I stared at him. "What did you say?"

"You heard me."

I stood with my mouth open as if I were screaming in a dream.

He gripped my arm. "Now let's just quiet down. You and I are going back to the table and we're going to sit down and eat our dinner," he said, steering me into the dining room.

I pulled away, heading for the door.

He blocked my way.

I dashed around him and opened the door, but he yanked me back, pushed me against the wall and pressed the open door against me.

"Nate. Let me go," I said as quietly and carefully as if I were negotiating with one of those crazy hostage-takers holed up in a house. His behavior had crossed some kind of line from intimidating to absurd and the more he raged, the calmer I felt. I knew what I had to do. It was as simple as that. There was no contest.

Pinned against the wall, still clutching the wrapped food, I waited.

"Go to hell," he muttered abruptly, opening the door and knocking the food out of my hand. The jar crashed and shattered, spilling the jello, but I retrieved the meatloaf and the baked potato, and left the house.

When I let myself into my mother's apartment with my key, she wasn't sitting in the living room waiting for me as usual. She wasn't in the bedroom, either, and the kitchen was deserted. I felt a stab of panic—I had been so late she tried to get to the hospital by herself and collapsed somewhere.

I pounded on the bathroom door. "Mom! Are you in there!"

"I'm in the tub," she said.

"You're in the tub! What're you doing in the tub! You're expected at the hospital!"

"I'm not going."

"What do you mean you're not going! You have to go!" I went into the bathroom. She was lying in the tub, her skin pale and puckered, her nipples flattened against her chest as if bound there by the death growing within her veins. Remembering her spongy, alive breasts and ripe torso, I looked down at a stranger's shrunken body.

"I can't stand it any more," she said. "I can't stand the tubes, the hospital, the food, the smells. Those goddamn nurses. It's enough. So I'll be anemic. I'm not going."

"So what did you call me for!" I said, exasperated, thinking of my fight with Nate.

"I just wanted to see you," she said in a small voice.

"Okay, I'm here. So get out of there." I held my hand out to help her but she waved me away and climbed unsteadily out of the tub. I handed her a towel. Smelling of Ivory soap, she wrapped herself in it and went into the bedroom.

Waiting in the living room, I picked up her *Time* magazine. The next-door neighbor's TV was on. Dinah Shore.

When she came into the room she was dressed in her good navy blue suit. She looked better. She had even put on lipstick.

"I brought you some meatloaf," I said, getting up.

"I'm not hungry."

"Okay, they'll give you something at the hospital. Let's go."

"You heard me. I'm not going."

"*Do as you're told,*" I said sharply. I had never spoken to her like that in my life.

She looked at me helplessly. Then she went to the closet and obediently put on her coat.

We had changed places.

Driving to the hospital, I took her hand. She pulled it away as if she recognized my touch for what it was— a gesture of pity that confirmed what must have been her increasing fear of what her "anemia" really was. And what lay ahead. She moved over to the window and turned away.

I never knew if she actually figured out what she had, but I think at this point we were both pretending for each other. I understand now that it would have been better if we had faced her approaching death together, but back then doctors didn't tell their terminal patients the truth; it seemed that pretending she would recover was the most we could do for her. Besides, while acting as if she would get better, I could almost believe it. That is, until I was alone. And driving home after leaving the hospital that night, I wept for her life and her death. Maybe she did, too.

I usually found her sitting up in a chair after a transfusion, but when I came to see her the next afternoon she was lying in bed. Trapped by her own blood and the tubes going in and out of her body, she was as white as the pillow under her head, her skin almost transparent, almost ethereal. There was an untouched plate of macaroni and cheese and a cup of tea gone cold on the tray that rolled up over the bed.

"Hi," I said. "How did it go?"

"I don't want that sandwich," she said, eying the deli bag I was holding. Her lips had a blue cast.

"Try just a bite," I said, unwrapping it. "Ham and cheese."

She knocked it out of my hand. "Get it away from me."

That was more like it. That was my mom. Her anger made me feel better. She was mad. I didn't blame her. When the nurse, then the head nurse, then the intern, then the resident, then Dr. Weisberg had tried to remove her dentures she raised so much hell it began to dawn on them that short of losing a finger there was no way they'd get my mother's false teeth out of her mouth.

I picked the sandwich up from the floor and put it in the waste basket.

"I'm sorry," she whispered. "I'm so sorry." Fear filled her wasted body and the hospital room. The air was thick with her fear. I remembered the blue fire of her eyes; now, her meek apology and unfocused gaze and childlike helplessness made me feel worse than the specter of her death. People die—parents die—but this slow ebbing, leaking, of the person who was my mother drove me out of the room into the corridor. I leaned against the wall trying to compose myself.

"I had to go to the ladies' room," I said when I returned.

"Joan called this morning," she said.

Joan was her boss. "What did she say?"

"She fired me."

So that was it. "Well, you've had to take a lot of time off lately."

"That kid was getting on my nerves anyway. I wasn't hired to be a babysitter."

I sat down. The room was the pale green color of an under-ripe avocado. There was a bed, a television anchored to the wall, the stiff chair I was sitting on. Fluorescent tubes cast an ugly green light. A man across the hall was talking loudly on the telephone, asking for his pajamas and vegetable soup. There was a soft murmur of voices in the corridor. A doctor imparting bad news? Was someone crying or did I imagine it? A cart rattled by. My mother lay with her eyes closed.

I was her only visitor during her hospitalizations. Kenny came when he could, but he lived 500 miles away. Except for the time Nate brought her that milk-shake, he stayed away, and her remaining sister, Lill, lived in Boston. Because of the guilt, finger-pointing and enmity that began with the murders, she had no relationship with her in-laws. And as Nate frequently pointed out, she was a woman who never kept a friend. One night I dreamed I was the only pallbearer at her funeral.

I thought she had fallen asleep, but as I tiptoed toward the door she opened her eyes.

"Are you leaving?" she asked pitifully.

"I have a dentist appointment." It was a lie. I had to get out of there. Sometimes I made up an appointment just to get away. Or I'd be grocery shopping or at school and suddenly want it to be over. I'd want her to die. Then I'd rush to the hospital, terrified that she was dead, that I had killed her with my mean wish, my selfishness.

I put on my coat. "You'll feel a lot better tomorrow after a good night's sleep," I said, sounding absurd even to myself.

"Dr. Weisberg looked grave when he was here this morning."

"Oh, that's just Dr. Weisberg," I said, cheerfully. "He always looks grave." I leaned over and kissed her. "See you later, Mom."

She closed her eyes and didn't answer.

I got into the elevator with five or six other people, each of us leaving a sick husband or wife or parent. We all turned and faced the door staring straight ahead as if we were riding alone, as if eye contact or words would expose our mix of grief, relief, terror.

Leaving the parking lot, I drove up Cedar Hill, heading home. But when I reached our driveway I kept on going, driving aimlessly, thinking of nothing. Finally, I turned back and parked at Shaker Lakes. Turning off the motor, I rolled the window down; it was an unseasonably warm day in December. The sun was low now, and the graceful trees bordering the lake cast deep shadows over the water. Gazing out of the window I noticed a couple strolling along holding hands and thought of Nate trying to stop me from taking my mother some meatloaf. The man and his small daughter feeding the ducks reminded me of my lost father; then I thought of the person who took my place on Dr. Herman's couch. A family in a station wagon pulled up in front of me and parked. As the children and their parents piled out, I thought of my mother wasting away in her hospital bed. Then I saw an old woman trudge along the path that bordered the lake. Dressed in ragged clothes, she was by herself and she looked so out of place in this elegant neighborhood I couldn't stop staring at her. That was me years from now, that was me, now. Alone.

When I came back that evening, I found my mother on the floor. She was dead. In a last burst of courage she died trying to do something as ordinary and monumental as get to the bathroom by herself.

I screamed for the nurse, who came running. The two of us lifted her cold body from the floor. It felt light. Laying her on the bed I saw the beauty in her still face, as if she were just pretending, playing dead as a joke, and would leap up, scaring me and making me laugh in relief and dread.

"I should have been here!" I sobbed to the nurse. "She shouldn't have died all alone on the floor!"

"I tried to take her to the bathroom," the nurse said. "She wouldn't let me. She told me to get the hell out. Among other things."

I was still weeping but I had to smile. That was my mom.

The nurse left the room and I sat down beside her. She was wearing her good nightgown as if she knew she was going to die that night and wanted to look her best. I told her what I wished I had said when she was alive. Speaking into the stillness, a stillness like nothing I had ever felt before, I told her that I loved her. That whatever had kept her in a grip of silence about my father and her other secrets came from places and people and events that were not of her doing. I said I understood what goes into survival isn't always pretty, and that I forgave her for my childhood. I said goodbye, feeling like the little daughter I had been when she was a gossamer, transparent goddess, leaving me lost and bereft in her absence, restoring me to life with her return. Now, except in my dreams, she would not be back.

Twenty-Six

WE BURIED HER with all the rituals. Our country club friends came to the funeral in their somber, elegant clothes. The rabbi spoke, although in generalities and cliches, as if he didn't know her, which of course he didn't—she hadn't attended a religious service for fifty years—not since she lived in the Home. After the services, we came back to the house for the traditional meal of smoked salmon and smoked whitefish, cream cheese, bagels, herring, hard boiled eggs, and pastries. The rabbi came, too, and said a prayer. We sat *shiva* for a week. Murmuring condolences, our relatives and friends came to pay their respects, and as was traditional, took turns bringing dinner to our house. Six feet under, my mother was suddenly the focus of the Jewish conventions and rituals she had shunned with contempt all her life. She would have loved the attention, and imperiously dismissed the rest of it as utter nonsense.

I knew my mother's height (five feet four) weight (125) and dress size (10). I knew her shoe size (7) and her politics and her favorite operas and books. I knew she had chronic indigestion and always ordered a vegetable plate in a restaurant. I knew what triggered her asthma, where she got her clothes dry cleaned and shoes repaired. I knew she snacked on strawberries standing over the sink, read *Time* magazine and the *Plain Dealer* from cover to cover and could type 65 words a minute. But my father was merely a figment of my imagination, a vapor. My mother had gone to her grave without having uttered his name for 40 years, and growing up without any real knowledge of him had made me feel lopsided and untethered. His absence was not simply a void as I had thought, it was as if I had been in the presence of a vacuum with the force of a wind tunnel.

So when I packed up her apartment after the funeral, I harbored a small hope that I would find among her things something of my father. Or of her secret life. A journal. A letter or two. A legal document or a scribbled telephone message. A revealing bill or canceled check. A telegram or an invitation or a photograph. But as if her staying hand had reached up from the grave, her resistance to my curiosity and need to know remained as stubborn and fierce as during her lifetime. I found nothing.

After the funeral, after the last caller left our house, after Goodwill had emptied my mother's apartment and life had returned to normal, her death began to surprise me. I half expected the car coming into my driveway to be hers, and when I answered the ringing telephone I thought she'd be there, sucking me back into her life. Sometimes it seemed as if I had made her death up out of frustration. Or that I was a small child again and she was too young and strong to die.

During her illness I had tried to imagine my life without her in it, but I had no idea how much I would miss her. I missed the timbre of her voice, her articulate opinions. Her brilliance. I even missed her illness. Taking care of her, avoiding her, worrying about her, complaining about her, blaming her, had structured my days and crowded out what was going on in my own life.

For a while I waited for the world to sort itself anew and my out-of-focus life in it. Then, slowly, cautiously, tentatively, I realized I could find out who I was without the threat of her ownership pulling at my sleeve, making me furious, making me proud, demanding attention, soaking up the precious oxygen of my days with her intense proximity. I realized that her death had left a void I could fill with a life of my own. I thought of the analysis I had fled. I told myself then that discovering a mind and vocation was enough, but now I wanted more.

I was greedy for more. I wanted to live without fear and self-contempt. Without misery. I wanted to get rid of whatever it was in myself that was making me unhappy and confused. It was time to go back to Dr. Herman, to the connection to myself I had fled. I had work to do. I was ready. Something felt like unfinished business. I didn't know then that it was divorce.

Twenty-Seven

"WELCOME BACK," DR. Herman says.

He looks the same and the office is so unchanged it feels like coming home. But now I have the coveted nine o'clock hour. I plop down on the couch as if I had left yesterday instead of two years ago.

He sits, waiting.

"My mother died," I say.

"Oh, I'm so sorry."

"Leukemia."

"When?"

"Four months ago."

Silence.

"Christ," I say, "I'd forgotten how irritating you can be."

"You're supposed to do the talking, remember?"

"I know," I sigh. "But it's been so long I don't know where to begin."

"Begin with what brings you back. Begin with the problem."

I smell Old English aftershave on the couch. The 8 o'clock hour's busy CEO with a sex problem? A student in mortal conflict with his father? No more Shalamar. I wonder if the Shalamar girl did better than I when she left. Or if she still comes at four o'clock.

"The problem?" I say. "The problem's me, the problem's Nate, the problem's I don't know. I left the analysis too soon. You were right. I should have listened."

"Maybe you weren't ready to listen."

I sigh. "Or to talk about my marriage."

"Yes," he says.

"I think I'm ready now."

"Go on," he says.

"Well, except that we fight more now, nothing's really changed. Nate still treats me like a two-year-old."

"Why did you pick that age?"

"Oh, for God's sake, Jake, it's just an expression. Sometimes a cigar is just a cigar."

"How old were you when your father was killed?"

"Two," I say.

"Yes," he says.

"So what am I to make of that?"

"What do you think?"

"There you go again," I groan. "I don't know! You're supposed to be the doctor!"

"You said Nate treats you like a two-year-old—your age when your father was killed."

"So?"

"So you picked an age that represents a time of extreme trauma in your life. You were two-years-old, before speech, before comprehension—a time when trauma has no place to go but underground. Where it lies while the unconscious mind tries to deal with it."

"Well, my unconscious mind isn't dealing with it very well."

"Of course not. It can't. By definition. It's unconscious."

"So, what can?" I ask.

"Making the unconscious, conscious."

"How do I do that?"

"By dredging up and then free-associating your true feelings in here."

"My true feelings? My true feelings are I can't stand the way Nate treats me anymore. I can't stand it!"

"Do you tell him how you feel?"

"God yes. Over and over. I tell him all the time. I threaten to leave. I have left. But he always knows how to get me back . . . then he behaves better for a while . . . but it never lasts and we go round and round and I'm sick of it . . . I'm so sick of it . . . I know he'll never change and I always forgive him."

"Why do you think?"

"Why do I think what?"

"Why do you think you always forgive him for what you say you can't stand?"

"I don't know! That's why I came back!"

He is silent.

I close my eyes. It has started to rain and I hear a faint rumble of thunder in the distance.

He sits behind me, waiting. I listen to a murmur of voices in the dentist's office next door, trying to make out the words. A telephone is ringing somewhere.

"Go on," he prompts.

"All I seem able to do is daydream about leaving," I sigh.

"Tell me what you think of when you imagine leaving Nate."

"Imagine? I said I daydreamed."

"What's the difference?"

"Daydreaming's like fantasy. Like how great it will be," I say. "Imagining is what it'll really be like."

"And what will it really be like?"

"Getting swallowed up by my mother," I say, surprising myself.

"But she's dead."

"You know," I say, "she's been dead for over four months and I swear to God I keep forgetting it. It's like she couldn't really be dead. Not *her*."

"Or that she's so powerful and omnipotent she'll swallow you up from the grave?"

I shudder and lie there listening to the drumbeat of rain against the window.

"What else do you imagine?" he finally asks.

"Oh, you know—the usual, being out there—dating."

"How does that feel?"

"Exciting. Scary. I've never had sex with anyone but Nate."

"What's the scary part?"

I close my eyes, trying to think. What *am* I afraid of? Haven't I been on my own since I was six years old? A street-smart kid? Why should I be afraid now. I'm a grown woman now. And then I know. That's it. I'm a grown woman. I remember the dream of being naked with Nate's cameo around my neck. I sit straight up on the couch.

"I'm afraid of losing Nate's protection," I say.

"What kind of protection?"

"Sexual."

"Yes," he says. "Growing up you had no one to protect you either from the sexual assault of strangers or from your own developing sexuality. Nate's oppression and control that you complain about was just what you wanted—the protection you needed as a child and never had. So now when you think of being without him, in your unconscious mind you're still a frightened, vulnerable, defenseless child."

"But I've grown up."

"The unconscious mind has its own calendar."

That night I hurry to bed while Nate is in the shower, pull the covers over my head and shut my eyes hard. I hear the bathroom door open and then feel the mattress sag a little as he climbs into bed. I turn away. Naked, smelling of soap, he kisses my neck and reaches for my breast. His mouth and hands had always aroused me, but now his arms feel like a vise and when he tries to turn me over I am afraid I'll start screaming. Feeling his hot breath on my skin, feeling chained to the bed, to Nate, I leap out. Choking, breathing, my eyes and nose dripping, I go into my dressing room and lie down on the curved Louis XV sofa.

I had left my husband's bed for this small, stiff couch. Feeling delivered, feeling frightened, I lie there listening to him furiously pace the bedroom, surprised at my audacity, surprised at my exhilaration, feeling suddenly, unaccountably free on this hard-edged couch with my feet hanging over the edge.

Every morning at nine o'clock I return to Dr. Herman. I feel as if I am being raised anew, going through my life again, out of time, in the benign soil of a hothouse (this dim room, this couch). Dr. Herman is the gardener helping me pull out the choking weeds of my childhood, releasing my unconscious mind of its burdens and conflicts, giving me a second chance at growing up.

I am a child on the couch, but I am also old, ancient in my youth, looking over my shoulder at those years, reliving the deaths, the little daily deaths and the huge eternal deaths; this time feeling them, freeing unshed tears, falling into the abyss of tears, safe, guided by Dr. Herman behind me and my mysteriously knowing, unconscious self. It is like excavating through layers and layers until I reach the person, me, who has been there all along.

Twenty-Eight

THIS TIME I decided to go to the best. The attorney at his desk across from me was head of the most prestigious law firm in Cleveland, a former campaign manager of a United States Presidential candidate, well-known for his social consciousness and high-placed corporate, political and eminent clients. I would never have been able to get an appointment with him if I hadn't done volunteer work on a project dear to his heart: The United World Federalists, an international organization working toward achieving world peace through world law.

"What does your husband say about this divorce?" he asked.

"He doesn't want it," I said.

He sat back in his chair, frowning. "Babette, I have to tell you. If he contests you have no grounds."

"What do you mean no grounds! You know how he treats me." He had caught me weeping one day after a meeting and asked what was wrong.

"Yes, but I'm afraid it will come down to your word against his. Do you have any bruises?"

"Bruises? Yeah, but they don't show."

"Well, what about witnesses?"

I shook my head. "We were always alone."

"Then he can either refuse the divorce or make the terms too unacceptable."

"Okay, we'll take him to court."

"I don't advise it."

"Why!"

"Because as I said, it will be his word against yours. Your husband's a pillar of the community. The judge will almost certainly be a man. Who do you think he'll believe? A court battle could take years and you could still lose. You probably would." He gazed at me across the desk. "What work background do you have? Besides your volunteer work, what are your skills?"

"Skills?"

"Yes, my dear. Skills. To earn a living."

I shook my head. All I'd ever done is model clothes and even if anyone would still hire me, how long could I do that?

"Babette," he said, sighing, "I'm going to say something you won't want to hear. Nate Hoffman is a very well-known, wealthy and powerful man. He doesn't want a divorce. You have three children and no way to support yourself. Go home and work out your problems with him." He shook his head. "I'm sorry to have to say this but you have little choice. Have your tried a marriage counselor?"

"He refuses to go."

"Well, you'd better give this some very careful thought. Is there someone you can talk to? Family? Friends? If you decide to go through with this you'll need their support."

But I didn't get any. As the lawyer reminded me, no one I knew understood why I'd want to leave this rich man, provider of luxuries, self-proclaimed perfect husband. Dr. Herman refused to give me advice, and every time I tried to talk to Nate he either shouted me down or turned a deaf ear. I didn't know what to do. Drifting in a kind of limbo, I grieved as if someone were dying.

As if it were me.

I was dying.

"Nate," I said in a small voice. "Please. Give me a divorce."

We were sitting in the den. The children were in bed.

"Not that again," he groaned behind his newspaper.

"Please," I said again. "Nate. Put the paper down. Talk to me."

He folded the paper slowly, deliberately, as if it were some kind of priceless document and laid it in his lap. "You know what? I'm sick of your whining. All you do is kvetch. It's enough already. I told you before. No divorce."

"But I can't live like this. I can't."

"Poor you. Poor, poor you," he whimpered, imitating my pitiful voice. "Poor you can't live like this. Two maids, a yacht, this house, everything I buy you—the furs, the jewelry. How can you stand it. Boohoo boohoo," he sniffled, mimicking the tears that were now streaming down my face.

I reached for my handkerchief and wiped my eyes. "It's not that, it's the way you treat me—"

"Yeah, you're mistreated. You know what? You're crazy. You're really nuts," he said, picking up his newspaper.

"So if I'm so crazy why do you want to stay married to me?"

"Because you're my wife. Because we have children. Now please shut up already so I can read."

I stared at the newspaper covering his face. I could read the headlines: . . . U.S. bombers attack Hanoi . . . Spencer Tracy dies . . . something about the Shah of Iran. The room was quiet, then the grandfather clock in the foyer chimed ten times. Soon it would toll eleven times and then twelve; then bed at Nate's side where I had returned to keep the peace, and then morning and another day and another one after that, with my life drifting away like sand while the clock rang the hours as an ominous prophecy.

Then something happened. Mysteriously, magically, I began to feel my mother's spirit from the grave or the air or my own heart, and I clutched her legacy of

220

courage like an heiress or thief. Her shining example of valor under conditions that made mine look easy lifted my head and straightened my spine where I sat.

"I'm going to do it," I said to Nate's newspaper. "This time I'm going to do it."

There must have been something new in my voice because I got his attention. He thrust the newspaper aside and glared at me. "What did you say?"

"I said I'm getting a divorce. I said this time I'm going to do it."

"The hell you say."

"You can't stop me."

"That's what you think," he said. "Watch me."

I stood up. "Talk to my lawyer."

He jumped out of his chair and lunged forward. "I'll break you!"

I turned my back and leaving the room, looked over my shoulder. He was standing there with his mouth open and his hands hanging limply at his side looking as astonished and red-faced and helpless as if he believed me.

Twenty-Nine

"I'M READY," I told the lawyer.

"Did your husband change his mind?"

"No."

"Babette, I can't advise this."

"Okay, you warned me," I said.

He narrowed his eyes and gazed at me for a long moment. "You seem different. What happened?"

"I think it was my mother."

"Your mother? You came into some money from your mother?"

I shook my head. "She died."

"I don't understand."

"Neither do I," I said, smiling.

He leaned foreward. "As I told you, you're in a no-win situation, so you'd better make absolutely sure you want to start this."

"I'm sure."

He appraised me. "You understand it won't be easy. You understand the probability of a drastically reduced income and lifestyle."

"Yes," I said. "I understand."

He looked at me hard. "You must really want this."

"John, one way or another I'm going to get this divorce. I need you to help me because I trust you. But if you won't do it I'll find someone who will."

He leaned back in his chair, put his hands behind his head and stared out the window.

I watched him, waiting.

After a while he picked up the phone. "Ginny, hold my calls."

"So John. Are we going to do it?"

He sat forward. "Yes ma'am. We're going to do it."

In the end Nate knew he couldn't stop me because I had lost my fear. In the end Nate knew he couldn't stop me because I discovered that if you scratch a bully there's no blood. In the end he knew—he had to know on some level—that it was he who destroyed our marriage. And six weeks later I emerged, blinking in the light, as if I'd been jailed and then handed a reprieve from a mysterious crime I did not know I committed. And I was free.

I want to give Dr. Herman something for helping me stop the steam roller that my father had started, my mother had fueled, and Nate had damn near driven over me. I finally settle on a silver desk set engraved with his monogram. I give it to him at our last session. It is beautifully wrapped. He doesn't open it. He thanks me. I want to hug him but we shake hands, and I leave. My eyes are so wet I bump into someone in the corridor.

Thirty

NATE GAVE ME the furniture he didn't want. The movers loaded the last of it from the big house into the truck and backed out of the driveway. The living room, the family room, the grand dining room, the library, looked barren without their paintings and brocades and silks. Smaller, somehow.

The country club gossip was that I had fallen in love with another man. But it wasn't some grand passion that broke up our marriage, like Anna Karenina's or Emma Bovary's. It was my own lost and found self. Still, walking through the empty rooms where so much damage was done by Nate, by my breaking away, by the divorce, I mourned my home and marriage as if someone had died.

But amidst the awesome weight of love for my children and guilt for breaking up their home, I felt a wave of serenity that was so pleasurable and flooding, it startled me. I didn't know, of course, what lay ahead — freedom or loneliness, autonomy or poverty. I didn't know yet of the wonderful man I would meet and love, or the happy marriage we would make. Feeling something that might have been excitement or might have been fear, it was as if the future slipped into this house like a phantom, unknown and dangerous and thrilling.

Through the kitchen window I saw fat snowflakes as bright as diamonds float to the ground, illuminating the stiff plants and ground with an iridescent glow. Now, stripped of its life, the rooms were turning dark and chilly, and the air smelled damp, as if emptiness had an odor. I put on my coat. It was time to leave for the apartment I had rented. The moving van was on its way, my rooms swept clean, and waiting.